CONVERSATIONAL COMMENTARY ON

PHILIPPIANS

A Life of Joyful Endurance

BY MICHELLE MYERS

SWHW
SHE WORKS HIS WAY

Conversational Commentary onPhilippians
A Life of Joyful Endurance

©2023 Myers Cross Training
His Way Resources, Inc.
Design + Layout ©2023 Erica Zoller Creative, LLC

ISBN 9798396698932

CONTENTS

CONVERSATIONAL COMMENTARY ON PHILIPPIANS:

Acknowledgments

My Bible margins are filled with notes I've written over the years -- a combination of sermons heard and books read, lecture notes during seminary, insights from countless discipleship groups, retreats and conferences, as well as my own personal study. To all who have used your gifts as stewards of God's grace, I am forever grateful for your investment in my life and the lives of many others.

Paul's relationship with the Philippians reminds me of the couples in our first small group when James and I were newlyweds. Whether it's an intentional in-person visit or our active group text, 16 years later, we can still count on these friends to point back to the joy we have in Jesus. **_Tim + Meagan Bergeron and Alan + Candice Armstrong_**, James and I are so grateful to God for you.

- Michelle Myers

Introducing Conversational Commentary

Some of my favorite moments take place in church or a living room with other women gathered around an open Bible. It's during those moments when I see for myself that God's Word is living and active *(Hebrews 4:12)*, when I'm taught by older women and am able to teach younger women, and when that teaching isn't merely done with words but is coupled with an example *(Titus 2:1-5)*.

So when God first began stirring this series in my heart, I wondered if it would be possible to create a gospel-centered conversation that would take place inside gospel community -- not just writing content. Because this world is not lacking in good -- *yes, even gospel-centered* -- information. We also have more distribution channels to provide the information to more people in ways that are quick, cost-efficient, and convenient to access. I'm grateful for these outlets. Any place the gospel can be proclaimed is reason to rejoice. But the good information and great distribution are not enough on their own. As believers, we're *all* called to be disciples who make disciples -- and that cannot be automated and distributed, delegated to some, or designed for the masses.

So that's where the idea of writing conversational commentary began. God's Word is God speaking to us, we get to continue the conversation He started in the commentary, and the corresponding questions enable you to build discipleship relationships with women you know.

WHAT TO EXPECT: GOSPEL-CENTERED CONVERSATION

When I'm doing a deep dive into a particular book, I have between 6-10 resources that I dig into that range from study Bibles and concordances to theological dictionaries and systematic theology books. *(See the back for my reference guide of my favorite Bible study tools.)* In this series, the goal is to supply enough historical context and theological explanation for deep understanding without crossing over into so much head knowledge that it distracts from the main message of the gospel. Should you come across something "missing" in the commentary, that likely means we felt elaborating on it would divert the conversation into secondary issues that too often divide rather than unify.

There's also a reason we chose to call this *conversational* commentary: because I want you to feel like you're sitting in my living room with a cup of coffee and an open Bible. The verse-by-verse commentary is anchored in truth about God, but His truth also invites us to lovingly respond. I loved the opportunity to include in the commentary how God has moved in my heart to obey the truth in the text.

WHAT TO EXPECT: COMMENTARY BY WOMEN FOR WOMEN

While my being a woman does not change the truth written in God's Word, it does affect my perspective, what obedience practically looks like, and the roles and experiences God has given me in my life. While these conversations and questions could absolutely be used in mixed-gender settings, I wanted to provide commentary and questions that specifically address God's design for women as well as women's roles as partners in the gospel, wives and moms -- among many others. God's Word has shaped how I see every role in my life and every place He has called me. I pray this series equips women to fulfill the Great Commission *(Matthew 28:19-20)* and to see their valuable place in God's work in the world.

WHAT TO EXPECT: MULTIPLICATION THROUGH DISCIPLESHIP

In the last letter he wrote before he was killed, Paul gave Timothy some descriptors of the Lord's servant, one being *"able to teach" (2 Timothy 2:24)*. Paul is not advocating to Timothy that all of God's servants must be skilled communicators, but that they must *know the* truth so they can *teach* the truth to others. Some have long regarded teaching merely as a spiritual gift. And while God has certainly given some the gift of teaching, teaching is more than a gift. Teaching cannot be separated from discipleship. You wouldn't have this book in your hand if you didn't feel called to know God more through His Word. But what you are compelled to *know*, you should also be compelled to *share.*

WHAT TO EXPECT: GROUP DISCUSSION QUESTIONS

Along with commentary for verse-by-verse study, I've included questions for group discussion. I've done my best to follow a formula my husband *(one of the most passionate people about discipleship that I know)* calls *peeling the onion* -- a method where the questions require more thought and transparency the deeper into the discussion you go. Specifically, each discussion begins with an icebreaker that is based on personal experience. Next, there are 2-4 questions with answers that are relatively simple to find right there in the text. Finally, the discussion concludes with another 2-3 questions that require more personal reflection, accountability and application.

If you have a spiritually mature group, you may not need to use the provided questions at all. These open-ended questions could work to guide a great discussion for each meeting:

1. *What stood out to you most? Did you notice anything for the first time?*
2. *What did this text prompt you to pray for/about?*
3. *Based on what you read, what action do you need to take in your life to obey what you learned?*

A note of encouragement: The discussion will get easier as your group meets with more frequency. It's normal for conversation to be quieter in the beginning, so don't be discouraged if it feels like you're doing a lot of the talking when your group is new. Make it your goal to talk less each week and make sure you're waiting long enough after you ask a question before you jump in to answer it yourself. Moments of silence feel longer when you're the one initiating the conversation – so be okay with a few pauses in conversation. Someone will jump in eventually, and the silence gaps will get shorter as your group becomes more comfortable with one another.

As noted at the beginning, though, discipleship is not merely words. Bringing people in closer to you will provide you with opportunities to demonstrate the gospel through your care for them and your actions in general. These moments are not secondary to your time spent teaching. Take the time to love deeply. As my pastor, Bruce Frank, says all the time, "Declare *and* demonstrate the gospel."

Praying for you and your group! May God speak powerfully to us through His Word.

In Him,
Michelle

Before You Read Philippians

The book of Philippians was written by Paul from a Roman prison around 62 AD. About 12 years has passed between the beginning of the church at Philippi *(approximately 50 AD)*, recorded in Acts 16. Though his stays were never long, Paul returned to Philippi on several of his missionary journeys, and the church at Philippi played a significant support role to Paul's ministry. Paul often wrote letters to the churches he helped start, but Philippians is unique in that it's the only letter he wrote that has far more encouragement than it does correction. The reminders Paul gave the Philippians are the same reminders we need today as we aim for spiritual maturity to live a life of joyful endurance.

As you read, here are some recurring themes to look for:

Christ-Likeness

Spiritual growth/maturity is not about how much Bible knowledge you have, how many mission trips you've been on, or how many church services you've attended. While those things are certainly valuable, the real mark of spiritual maturity is becoming more like Jesus. *(The fancy church word for this is sanctification.)* Christ-likeness, centering on Jesus' example, requires humility, obedience, and suffering. Jesus is our example, our strength, and our hope.

All throughout the New Testament, we see people who studied the Old Testament Scriptures intently. In fact, many of the Pharisees had the majority of the first five books of the Old Testament memorized. *(Can you imagine memorizing Leviticus?!)* But yet, when Jesus walked among them, they didn't recognize Him. The same tragedy is still possible today. We can sing songs, study Scripture, and know *about* God – but not really know Him.

As Paul points out throughout this letter, don't just stop at knowledge. Want more of Jesus – *not other things*. Rely on Jesus – *not other things*. Hope in Jesus – *not other things*. As He becomes your aim, you will become more and more in His likeness.

To evaluate if you are growing in Christ-likeness, here are three questions:

1. Are you growing in your dependence on the Lord?
2. Are you growing in your love for others?
3. Are you growing in confidence in what you have not yet seen?

Joyful Endurance

Philippians is often called Paul's joy letter. Paul mentions the idea of joy or rejoicing 16 times in just 104 verses *(1:25; 2:2; 2:17; 2:18; 2:28; 3:1; 4:1; 4:4; 4:10; 4:12)*. Paul constantly reminds the Philippians that joy comes through Jesus. Happiness in anything else will depend on circumstances, but what Jesus accomplished through His death and resurrection is final and forever. If what Jesus has done is the only good thing that ever happens to us, we still have more than enough reason to rejoice.

Despite the fact that Jesus provides us with nothing to fear and every reason to rejoice, if we take our eyes off Him and begin to long for the things this world has to offer, we can end up caught in the same hamster wheel as those who haven't heard the gospel – endlessly searching for meaning and joy here on earth. But if we keep our eyes on Jesus and participate in His mission, we have everything we need to live a life of *joyful* endurance.

Endurance often comes with a mindset of just putting your head down and getting through it. But through Jesus, our Heavenly Father has provided us a way to joyfully endure until we are with Him for eternity – even now.

In Philippians 2:2, Paul instructs the Philippians to complete his joy. As you'll be reminded as you read, this complete joy that Paul writes about is rooted in Jesus and continues God's mission alongside other believers.

Here are some questions to ponder if the joy you're experiencing is incomplete:
- Am I *wanting* something other than or in addition to Jesus?
- Am I *relying* on something other than or in addition to Jesus?

- Am I *hoping* in something other than or in addition to Jesus?
- Am I isolated or in community?
- Do I look out for myself or others first?

Loving Others through the Love of God

Whether in mindset or in action, we often separate the call to love God from the call to love others. Both matter, but we make distinctions between the two. Through his relationship with the Philippians, Paul demonstrates here what it looks like to love others *through* the love of God – both our love for God as well as His love for us. As you read, notice how Paul intertwines his love for the Philippians *(and their love for him)* with his love for the Lord. As you read, you'll find answers to these questions right there in the text:

1. How was their relationship formed?
2. Despite the distance between them, how much deeper does the relationship go with God's love as the foundation instead of feelings?
3. What fruit is produced from the relationship that impacts beyond Paul and the Philippians?
4. How do they maintain their relationship?

As you answer these questions, use what you learn to specifically pray for God to help you to love others through His love.

The Church at Philippi Snapshot:

✝ First church Paul started in Europe *(Acts 16)*

🏃 Roman colony known for patriotism to Rome

👯 Joyfully committed to Jesus and the gospel mission in the face of persecution

👪 Composed of a diverse group of individuals – Lydia - a rich business woman; converted jailer; former demon-possessed slave girl *(Acts 16)*

Paul Snapshot:

- Born as a Roman citizen and trained as a Pharisee

- Also known as Saul of Tarsus

- Persecuted Christians and participated in the martyrdom of Stephen (Acts 7)

- Converted to Christianity on the road to Damascus (Acts 9)

- Preached Christ faithfully for three missionary journeys

- Wrote letters to churches and believers that later became 13 books of the New Testament

- Worked as a tentmaker to financially support his ministry

- Remembered as the greatest missionary of all time and the apostle to the Gentiles

Philippians Fast Facts:

- Written around A.D. 61 from one of Paul's imprisonments in Rome

- Paul lists Timothy as a co-author

- Often known as Paul's joy letter; he uses the words joy or rejoice 16 times in just 104 verses

- Mainly written to Gentiles, so Paul did not directly quote the Old Testament in this letter (They didn't know it yet!)

Dig Deeper:
On the next page, you'll find bonus commentary of Acts 16. This passage records the start of the church at Philippi – the recipients of the letter to the Philippians. As we read Scripture, it deepens our understanding when we consider the context of the original audience. Before you dig into the contents of the letter to the Philippians, study this bonus excerpt originally published in *Conversational Commentary on Acts: Gospel Mission Then and Now.*

- Lord, speak to our hearts as we come to Your Word. Thank you for sending Jesus so we can joyfully endure until You return or call us home. Amen.

Acts 16

16:1　In his 2nd letter to Timothy, Paul expands on the faith of Timothy's mother and grandmother. Cross-reference to 2 Timothy 1:5.

16:3　Because Timothy grew up in the area where they were ministering, people knew his father was a Greek. Paul had Timothy get circumcised because he didn't want to waste energy on nonessentials of faith. Paul, like Timothy, grew up Jewish. He wasn't opposed to anything of Jewish tradition, like circumcision, except for the instances, like the Jerusalem Council, where people were adding to what was required for salvation. This is not people-pleasing or conforming to expectations, but removing obstacles so they could minister to people more effectively without distraction.

16:5　Luke frequently chronicles the growth of the church in Acts, but it's never simply about the numbers. Here, he notes how churches were strengthened in the faith, and because of their strengthened faith, they grew. Make strengthened faith the goal and trust God for numerical growth.

16:6-7　The Holy Spirit will guide you in what to do and what *not* to do. And it's not merely a matter of doing something right or doing something wrong, but the Holy Spirit can and will guide each of us personally. Here, Paul and Silas were forbidden and stopped by the Holy Spirit from going to certain cities to preach the gospel. It's not that preaching the gospel in those cities would have been wrong, but God had other plans for them of where He needed them to go. Pay attention to His guidance.

16:9-10　The vision was brief of a man asking for help in Macedonia, and they interpreted it to mean they needed to take the gospel to

Macedonia. As you help others, remember that the gospel is what both saves us and sustains us.

16:10   The pronouns *"we"* and *"us"* used here indicate that this was when Luke joined Paul on his second missionary journey.

16:13   It took 10 men to make a Jewish synagogue in a city, so that means in this area, there were less than 10 Jewish men since there was a place of prayer but no synagogue. They still stuck to their normal routine as best they could by going to the place of prayer to connect with people who were interested in spiritual matters.

16:13   Cultural boundaries would have prevented men and women from speaking to one another in public. However, just as Paul didn't let the cultural differences and subsequent boundaries stop him from sharing the gospel here, we shouldn't let them get in our way either.

16:14   God opened Lydia's heart to pay attention to Paul's words and to respond. Salvation is the supernatural work of God, not the persuasiveness or eloquence of the preacher. When you share the gospel, remember that it's not as much about your words or gift of speaking as it is about God's work in hearts.

16:15   It's not uncommon in the book of Acts to record that a person was saved along with their whole household. Even when an entire family is converted and shared as a unit, salvation is an individual decision. Lydia's conversion and baptism, along with the conversions and baptisms of her household, indicates that she shared the gospel with her family after she got saved.

16:15   Lydia blessed the apostles and the church with her gift of hospitality. [Acts 16:40 indicates that Lydia's home became the gathering place for the believers.] Open your home to others. The root word for hospitality in the Greek is the same as the word "hospital." In our world today, we tend to confuse hospitality with entertaining. Hospitality is about the guest, but entertaining usually makes the gathering about the host. Remove all of the Pinterest boards from your mind on what it means to be a hostess, and see your home more like a hospital instead. Is your home a place where hurting people can come and feel better when they leave?

16:16 The slave girl with *"a spirit of divination"* is another way to say this slave girl had a demonic spirit. She was a demon-possessed child, and instead of helping her, her owners were exploiting her pain for their own gain.

16:17 It's so interesting to think that the demons recognized Jesus as the Son of God, and yet, so many of the religious leaders did not.

16:18 Why was Paul greatly annoyed? Though her words were true, he probably did not want anyone to mis-associate her as being his ministry partner. Perhaps he was just righteously indignant that truth and evil do not mix. Or maybe because she kept saying the same phrase over and over for several days, he's finally just had enough.

16:18 Cross-reference to Matthew 8:16, Matthew 10:8, Matthew 12:28, and Luke 10:17. Jesus exercised His authority over demons while He was on earth, and He gave the same authority to His disciples as well. Rather than praying to God, Paul spoke directly to the demon and commanded it to come out in the name of Jesus. Paul's power or authority did not make the demon come out; the power and authority of Jesus did.

16:19 When money becomes a motivator, it often works against the gospel. We saw it already with the magician *(Acts 8:18-24)*, we see it here, and we'll see it again with the silversmith *(Acts 19:24)*. When profit matters more than God's glory, salvation, or what's best for others, money has become an idol.

16:19-24 Paul and Silas were falsely accused, stripped, beaten, and imprisoned without a fair hearing. Do not expect to be treated fairly when you live for Jesus. Expect increased opposition more than you expect fairness.

16:25 After being stripped, beaten, and imprisoned, Paul and Silas chose to praise God, and the prisoners paid attention. When your praise for God follows hardship, that's likely to be the time that most people will listen to you.

16:26-27 Prison guards who lost their prisoners were typically given the same sentence as the prisoner they lost. The jailer supposed that because he lost all of the prisoners, he was going to be killed anyway. The thing that I find the most intriguing in this miracle is not merely that Paul and Silas didn't escape, but that none of the other prisoners tried to escape either. This side of heaven, we'll never know why, but my best guess is that the prisoners were so curious about Paul and Silas' faith on display through their worship that they stayed to see what would happen next.

16:28-29 Just like people will listen if you praise God after hardship, they will also likely be curious about God if you care about someone who has treated you poorly. There's a good chance the jailer who is with them was also one of the men who beat them.

16:30 You never know who is listening to you or watching you. But because the jailer's question was about how he could be saved, we know he was listening to Paul and Silas' teaching or their worship.

16:31 Notice they told him to "believe *in*" the Lord Jesus, and not just to "believe *that*" the Lord Jesus... There is a difference between believing *in* Jesus and believing *that* Jesus. Put your full confidence in Jesus.

16:32-33 God can change people through the gospel. Hours before, the jailer inflicted wounds upon Paul and Silas. And now that he has learned of Christ, the jailer is washing their wounds. No one is too far gone for God to reach.

16:34 Joy and salvation go together. When you find yourself fighting for joy, recall the gospel. Remember what Jesus did for you. Reflect on your life before Christ and your life now. Our salvation should lead us to rejoice!

16:35-39 Paul is not trying to get justice for the way they were treated, but he is trying to make sure that their release is as public as their arrest. He didn't want others to falsely believe that Christianity was a threat to Rome, as they were accused. Paul wanted it to be clear a mistake was made to protect the future of the gospel and the witness of Christ. He is standing up for others who could be in their situation in the future.

16:40 Although they were probably physically sore from their beating and exhausted from not sleeping in prison, they prioritized making time to encourage the church at Philippi. As you read Philippians, picture some of the people introduced in this chapter that Paul would have been writing to – like Lydia, the slave girl and the jailer.

Philippians 1:1-11

COMMENTARY

1:1   While Paul is often referred to as the solo author, he frequently mentions co-authors of his letters, as he does here with Timothy. *(He also did this in 1 Corinthians, 2 Corinthians, Galatians, Colossians, 1 Thessalonians, and 2 Thessalonians).* Timothy, a young pastor, often traveled with Paul. Paul affectionately referred to Timothy as his spiritual son *(1 Timothy 1:2).* Paul describes their roles using the Greek word that is translated *"bond-servant."* The strong language used acknowledged the primary way Paul and Timothy identified themselves – not as missionaries, pastors or church leaders, but as the personal property of Jesus Christ. They also use intentional language to identify who they are writing to – *"the **saints** who are in Philippi, including the overseers and deacons."* It's not often that believers refer to one another as saints… but maybe we should! After all, believers are saints because of what Jesus has done, not anything we can do on our own. Here, *"saints"* is used as a reminder to the church at Philippi of the collective identity they have in their city – solely because of Jesus. Together, they are set apart for His Kingdom and His purposes in a particular place. I wonder if Paul added *"including the overseers and deacons''* to clarify so everyone in the church understood that it's not roles and responsibilities or how long you have or have not been walking with the Lord that qualify a person as a "saint." Believing in Jesus as your Lord and Savior does.

1:2   Between dwindling attention spans and the amount of viral marketing your normal day serves you, it would be easy to believe that in order to make a difference, you have to say something fresh and flashy. That's not the case when it comes to the gospel. Rather than needing something new, we need to be reminded of what we already have because of Jesus. That's what Paul does here. Grace and *"peace from God our Father and Lord Jesus Christ"* is not even something Paul is capable of giving them on his own. But even in Paul's absence, God's grace and peace were the reminders that the Philippians needed – and the reminders we need as well.

1:3-4   One of the main reasons Paul is writing this letter is because he's grateful for the money and supplies the Philippians sent with Epaphroditus for him. *(More on that soon!)* But rather than thanking them directly, Paul thanked *God* for what the Philippians had done. He recognized that ultimately, God was the One who moved the church at Philippi to be generous. I'm having to make some guesses here, but my assumption is that the reason why it was such a natural leap for Paul to thank God for His provision of what He supplied through the church at Philippi is because when Paul was in need, he didn't immediately go to the Philippians for help. Even though he knew some of them, like Lydia *(Read her story in Acts 16:11-15)* were financially well off and could easily provide for his needs, Paul didn't depend on believers who were financially able; he depended on God. Paul prayed God would meet his needs, and when the Philippians provided what he needed, Paul thanked God for His provision. And honestly, could there be greater encouragement for the Philippians than his words here? Imagine if someone told you, *"Whenever you come to mind – which is daily – I remember to thank God. Praying for you brings me incredible joy as I reflect on all those who have been impacted through the gospel since the first day we met."* That's what Paul is saying about the Philippians! It's easy to confuse encouragement with affirmation – but encouragement literally means "to put courage in." As believers, when we want to encourage one another, we need to say things that don't simply pat one another on the back, but actually stir one another up to put God's love and goodness into action *(Hebrews 10:24-25)*.

1:5   As I'm writing this, my daughter entrusted her life to Christ a week ago. When I say her excitement for the gospel is fresh, I mean she tapped me on the shoulder at 2am on the morning of her baptism and whisper-yelled in my ear, *"Jesus died on the cross for my sins, and that's why I'm getting baptized today!"* She didn't walk anywhere yesterday – she skipped. To top the day off – when we went to a Christmas party for our church's student ministry last night, the girl that would usually hold on to my leg so she could pretend to be shy and avoid having to talk to people became the queen of the dance floor. But Shea wasn't the only one who was excited about the gospel this week. Her excitement trickled to everyone in our home, reminding all of us of the joy of our own salvation. That's similar to what was happening in Philippi. Despite persecution, the church is still growing, and people are still coming to know Christ. The gospel stayed fresh on their minds because they were constantly sharing it with others who were hearing and believing for the first time. Excitement for the gospel doesn't require that you wake anyone up at 2am, but Jesus did tell us as His final command that as we go, we are to make disciples *(Matthew 28:19-20)*. Keep participating in the gospel with the same passion and excitement you did on the day you first believed by telling others what Jesus has done for you and for them. One of the most powerful ways to deepen your own faith is by helping someone else take their first steps toward God.

1:6   God never starts a project He won't finish. As faithful as He was to knit you together in your mother's womb *(Psalm 139:13)*, give you purpose, hope and a future *(Jeremiah 29:11)*, and make a way for you to get back to Him through Jesus *(Hebrews 12:24)*, He will be faithful to keep working on His purpose for you until He calls you home. God's work *for* you began long before you were born, and His work *in* you began the moment you first believed. Spiritual growth is everything that happens next that acknowledges both what God *is* doing and *will* do – which activates our faith. Sanctification is a fancy church word that describes the process of becoming more like Jesus – and it is just that: a process. Sanctification doesn't happen overnight. It won't look the same for all of us or even go in the same order. Each of us will have different struggles and different strengths. But our goal is the same: to become more like Jesus. Here's where this can get tricky: sometimes, what God gives us to make us more like Jesus wouldn't be what we would choose for ourselves. Given the choice, we would likely never choose struggle, sacrifice or suffering. But living to be sanctified – to become more like Jesus – requires that we stop seeing things merely with human eyes as good or bad, but recognizing that everything we encounter in life is something God has either orchestrated or allowed that will provide us with an opportunity to become more like Jesus. In a sermon called *A Happy Christian*, Charles Spurgeon put it this way: *"The worldling* *blesses God while he gives him plenty, but the Christian blesses Him when He smites him: he believes Him to be too wise to err and too good to be unkind; he trusts Him where he cannot trace Him, looks up to Him in the darkest hour, and believes that all is well."* Trust God to be faithful to finish every good work He starts – including you.

1:7-8   What do you hold in your heart? For Paul, it was the grace of the gospel, which impacted the way he saw the people at Philippi. The people of this church were not perfect, but relationally, Paul leaned on their shared grace through God. Paul loved them through the love of Jesus, rather than mustering up his own affections, which is the deepest love we can experience as humans. When we love Jesus and meet others who love Him too, it unites us in a way that shared hobbies or merely a personality mesh cannot do. When I met my husband, I knew almost immediately that he was the man I was going to marry. It had nothing to do with love at first sight, but I recognized his love for Jesus, and I knew I wanted us to love Jesus together. It's the same kind of instant connection I feel when I get the opportunity to connect with women like you in person, or even just through an email. Even if we only interact through a brief exchange that lets me learn what God is doing in and through you, I mean it when I tell you that I love you and I'm grateful for you! That's what loving others with the affection of Jesus makes possible.

1:9   As backward as it may seem, given that Jesus said the greatest commandment is to love God and love others *(Matthew 22:37-40)*, love is rarely talked about as a key mark of spiritual maturity. However, spiritual maturity is exactly what Paul prays for here. Love is the anchor trait Paul begs God to increase *"more and more"* in the Philippians. Paul also prays that out of their growing love, *"real knowledge and all discernment"* will be produced. Real knowledge goes beyond simply what you know; it's acting on what you know to be true. Real knowledge is when your heart, your head and your hands are in agreement with what God has said and Jesus has done. In a similar way, *"all discernment"* is more than making wise decisions. Discernement is a willingness to yield to the Holy Spirit in all we do – in action *and* in motive. When you pray for spiritual growth in yourself and others, pray that love will continue to increase along with real knowledge and all discernment.

1:10   Why must our love abound with real knowledge and all discernment? Because until *"the day of the Lord Jesus"* when Christ returns for those who believe in Him, God has given each of us a life to live for His glory. God had His pick of how He would get the gospel message to the ends of the earth, but He chose us. Choosing what is *"excellent,"* means we will: 1) choose what is right over what is wrong *(or even the more challenging – choosing what is right over what is* almost *right!)*; 2) choose what matters for eternity over what "feels" like it matters right now; and 3) choose what God says over what simply sounds good. Yes, we have been saved by grace, not by our own good works *(Ephesians 2:8-9)*, but confessing Jesus as Lord means we've given God full control of our lives. Obeying God is not a performance, but it does prove our commitment to live for Him and His purposes is sincere, not just for sentimentality.

1:11   The previous two verses are packed with application: pursue abounding love, real knowledge, and all discernment *so that* how we live will be aligned with what we believe. But even in acknowledging his prayers for them, Paul reminds them that they don't have to muster this up in their own strength. This is not a checklist or a formula. It's a reminder that if you will fully depend on the Lord, He will give you what you need to live for Him. Paul's words here are similar to Jesus' own instruction to abide in Him so we will bear fruit *(see John 15:1-11)*. If this feels overwhelming to you, or even seems impossible, remind yourself regularly: this is the power of the gospel. You can't, but Jesus can. This is not about your ability to be perfect, but your privilege to be His. Rest in His power. Depend on Him for everything – because apart from Him, you can do nothing (John 15:5:). What a Savior! All glory and praise to God.

Philippians 1:1-11

QUESTIONS

Icebreaker: Who is someone you will forever be grateful to God for whenever you think of them? Share who they are and how God used them in your life.

1. Read Philippians 1:1 together. Paul uses intentional language to describe both himself and Timothy as well as the church at Philippi. What words does Paul use for each? Without getting caught up in semantics, do you think the words we use – both to describe ourselves and others – reveal more than we may realize? How would it change your perspective to think of yourself as Jesus' personal property and other believers as saints? What are other words you could use to describe yourself and others using the position we have in Jesus? What words unintentionally may deter you from remembering who you are in Christ?

2. In Philippians 1:2, Paul's first words do not offer the Philippians anything new, but remind them of what they already have – God's grace and peace. Do you feel pressure that you need to have something new to say to encourage those around you? Why do we struggle to see gospel reminders as what we really need? Spend a few moments encouraging each other by sharing gospel reminders that we really need.

3. Philippians 1:3-5 describes Paul's gratitude to God for how He provided for Paul through the Philippians. What's the significance in Paul saying he's grateful to God instead of being grateful for the Philippians? Practically, describe the difference between being grateful to God for how He uses others in our lives vs. just being grateful for what others do for us.

4. Philippians 1:5 implies the Philppians are still serving God with the same passion as they did when they first believed. Have a group member read Revelation 2:1-5 – a portion of a prophetic

letter to Ephesus which describes the opposite: a group of people whose love for the Lord dwindled over time. What do you think the differences are between participating in the gospel as you did on the first day vs. abandoning your first love? What are some ways we can prevent losing our enthusiasm for the gospel?

5. Philipians 1:7-8 describes how Paul loves the church at Philippi out of an overflow of his love for the Lord. What stands out to you from these two verses as reminders of how God makes it possible for us to love others through Him?

6. When you think of marks of spiritual maturity, where does love fall on your list? Does it surprise you that love is the trait Paul prioritizes in his prayer for the Philippians? Why or why not? What is the difference between the kind of love Paul writes about here and love that's merely a feeling? What's the difference between knowledge and real knowledge? What's the difference between all discernment and merely making wise decisions?

7. Read Philippians 1:9-11. How much comfort do you get that Jesus doesn't ask us to live this way apart from Him? As a group, discuss what it means to truly abide in Christ. How do you know for yourself when you are abiding in Christ vs. attempting to live for God on your own?

If you have a large group, break into groups of 2-3 people and end your group time by actually *putting courage in* one another. If your group is just getting to know one another, you may need to each share an area of your life where putting God first will require boldness and courage. Pray for one another specifically.

Philippians 1:12-30

COMMENTARY

1:12-13   Paul loved the Philippians, and they loved him too. It makes sense that they would be worried about him and the harsh conditions that prisoners often endured. But instead of egging on more empathy, Paul chooses to widen their perspective to help them see beyond his circumstance. Paul wants them to know that his imprisonment has allowed him to continue to advance the gospel. In Roman prisons, it was common practice for Paul to constantly be chained to a Roman guard. Paul chose to look past the chains and the armor to see a person who needed Christ and was actually *required* by his job to spend time with him. Because of the proximity he has to others, Paul reports that he has been able to share the gospel with everyone in the prison, including every member of the guard. Paul, a preacher of the gospel and a planter of churches, continued to preach and plant – right there in the midst of a terrible situation. His purpose didn't change in prison; prison simply became his pulpit. As followers of Christ, our purpose doesn't shift based on our situation. Refuse to let your circumstance distract you from the gospel. God can use you in His mission wherever you are. As Paul says, *"my imprisonment is for Christ,"* how would you personalize his words for yourself?

Fill in the blank below: **My _____ is for Christ.**

1:14   Paul's boldness for the gospel in prison inspired most of those who were free to be bold for the gospel as well. Hebrews 11:1 defines faith as *"the assurance of things hoped for, the conviction of things not seen."* Paul's faith – his hope and conviction of the gospel – inspired the faith of others. My pastor, Bruce Frank, often says, "The opposite of faith is not doubt; it's fear." This example illustrates his point so well. Fear typically paralyzes us from action, while faith produces results that only God can do. Exercise your faith – your confidence that God is bigger than whatever you fear – and God will use it for His glory and for good.

1:15   The same problem that existed then still exists now. Some people were preaching the gospel out of genuine calling and conviction. Others were preaching because they desired something for themselves – money, attention, some form of notoriety, etc. Others were jealous of Paul, so they viewed him as competition. I've said it before, and I'll say it again: There should be no competition whatsoever in the Kingdom. We have a shared mission, and God's in charge. As believers, we are called to function as Paul already said in Philippians 1:5 – as *partners* in the gospel. Allies, teammates, colleagues – whatever word makes the most sense to you – those are the kinds of words we should use to describe our relationship with one another.

1:16   General psychology indicates that human nature is most motivated by gaining incentives and minimizing loss. In other words, we aim to add pleasure and avoid pain. But Paul shares here that those who preached the gospel out of goodwill were motivated by love – which reflects Jesus' motivation. 1 John 3:16 reminds us, *"By this we know love, that he laid down his life for us, and we ought to lay down our lives for the brothers."* Let love – both for God and others – be your main motivation.

1:17-18   Paul is not dismissing wrong motives – and far more importantly than what Paul thinks, God does not excuse them either. Paul is simply releasing himself from the role of judge – which God has said is His responsibility alone *(See Hebrews 10:30)*. Paul's attitude is simply this: **If the gospel is advancing, I will rejoice.** I'm embarrassed to confess that I know firsthand that judging others is one of the quickest ways to lose your joy. It's hard to be joyful and critical at the same time. Again, this doesn't mean our motives don't matter or that we shouldn't speak truth over one another. But if keeping one another in line, so to speak, occupies your attention to the point where you do not rejoice in *(or are unaware of!)* the advancement of the gospel, those preaching the gospel for the wrong reasons aren't the only ones with misplaced motives: you've lost your way too. Regardless of who is preaching the gospel or why they are preaching the gospel, if God moves in someone's heart to take steps closer to Him, we should always be moved to rejoice.

1:19   When Paul refers to *"his deliverance,"* he's wrestling in his own mind how his imprisonment will end: whether he will be released and allowed to continue to minister or if he will be executed. But because of his faith in Christ and his confidence in the eternal life promised to him through Jesus, Paul sees *both* being freed from prison and death as God's deliverance. We often try to explain having an eternal perspective using words, but this may be one of the clearest examples we have from a human in Scripture: Paul sees death as much as God's deliverance as extended time on earth. Also, note that Paul indicates his deliverance will come through the Spirit of Jesus Christ *and* through the prayers of the Philippians. Prayer does not change God's plans. God is sovereign over all and has had a perfect plan from the beginning *(See Isaiah 46:9-10)*. However, our prayers are certainly part of God's plan. Prayer is part of how we are able to join God in His work in the world, and we should take our privilege to pray seriously.

1:20   This is a powerful sentence of faith. Not only is Paul waiting on God to act with *"eager expectation," "hope," and "full courage,"* but Paul is expressing unwavering confidence that God will get the glory, no matter what outcome He chooses. This is no simple circumstance either. Paul is expressing full trust through confident joy in Christ – whether he lives or dies. Have you ever found your faith being attached to a particular outcome – meaning your faith increases if how God moves aligns with how you think He should, and you find your faith dwindling if God acts in a way that you don't understand? As Paul models for us here, to stir up our faith, we should attach ourselves to being witnesses for Christ rather than desired outcomes.

1:21   A simple sentence with deep implications. *"To live is Christ"* implies that life means living for Christ's purposes. That's it. No earthly purpose will distract us or fulfill us. We are simply here for Jesus. *"To die is gain"* is just as powerful. Rather than fearing death, which is the leading fear of all humans, we get to view death as the end of our time in this broken world and the beginning of our life with Christ in His perfect Kingdom. There is no greater gain for a believer than the moment we will be face-to-face with our Savior.

1:22-24 It's typically entertaining, and yet somehow, enlightening, to review my notes in the margins of the Bible I used in middle school, which was when I began reading the Bible on my own. Scribbled next to these verses in a cross between a confession and desire for spiritual growth, I wrote, *"Not there yet."* Transparently, it was decades later before I read these verses and thought, "Same." But basically, Paul is continuing to wrestle here with how he wants to pray for himself and how he desires the Philippians to pray for him. He recognizes that life with Christ, away from the troubles of this world, finally free from all temptation and sin, is far greater than anything this world has to offer. As secure as Paul is in the safety of his salvation through Christ, though, Paul knows that it would be better for the Philippians, and for believers in general, if he is released so he can continue to minister and share the gospel. This insight allows us to see the struggle between flesh and spirit. But even in his spiritual maturity that recognizes Jesus is better, Paul's love for God spills over into how he loves others by being willing to sacrifice what would be best for him *(to die and be with Christ)* to do what is best for them *(to be released and continue the gospel mission on earth.)*

1:25-26 Convinced that it would be better for the gospel mission if he stayed, Paul is confident he will be released from prison. But note, Paul gives two reasons why he will remain to continue with them: 1) for their progress and joy in the faith, and 2) for all to give God the glory He deserves. First of all, I love that progress and joy are connected. As we grow in our faith, our joy should grow with it. It shouldn't be possible to grow in Jesus and get grumpy. But yet – the kind of unshakeable joy Paul writes about here is not common among Christians. It grieves me to admit, but simple observation suggests that believers gripe and complain as much as the person who is far from the Lord. It reminds me of the way Paul worded something in his letter to the Romans about Abraham. He wrote this: *"No unbelief made him waver concerning the promise of God, but he grew strong in his faith as he gave glory to God, fully convinced that God was able to do what he had promised"* (Romans 4:20-21). Knowledge *supports* growing faith for sure, but knowledge alone will not result in glorifying God. In fact, many times, increasing our knowledge often increases our confidence in ourselves – not in God. Here's the difference: growing faith will increase your confidence that God will always keep His promises. As your confidence in Him grows, so will a life of intimate and authentic worship. If you find yourself struggling for joy, examine your heart and ask God to reveal if you're truly progressing in faith or just in knowledge.

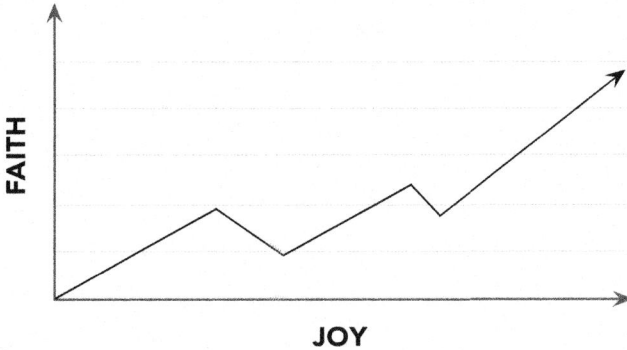

1:27   If you're an underliner or a highlighter in your Bible, *"only"* at the beginning of this verse would be a good word to emphasize for your memory. It's not just a matter of letting your life be worthy of the gospel of Christ, but *only* letting your life be worthy of the gospel of Christ. It's your sole aim. Paul further articulates what this looks like: 1) *"standing firm in one spirit;"* 2) *"with one mind;"* 3) *"striving side by side for the faith of the gospel."* Simply put, it looks like unity. In Philippians 4, we learn about some disunity that was happening among the Philippians, but before he gets specific, Paul reminds them to unite over the main mission and to save any fighting for the real opposition – not one another. Our unity – despite our differences – is one of the simplest ways to create curiosity among unbelievers. It won't happen unintentionally, which is why Paul calls us strongly to action to *"stand firm"* and to strive *"side by side."* When it comes to unity, are you standing firm, or are you unsteady? Are you striving alongside other believers, or are you isolated, coasting, or opposing them? God has been so good to give us the same mission. Let's aim to live in a way that remembers and reflects the gospel. Also, Paul's words here remind us that while we are not the judge of one another, we do need to hold one another accountable. Paul points out he will do this for the Philippians whether he is able to come and see them or he just hears of what's happening there. Accountability is not a matter of being *called out* for doing something wrong, but being *called up* to live worthy of the gospel. Who do you have in your life who calls you up?

1:28 Another reason why we shouldn't make enemies of one another is because we *do* have a real enemy. Opposition shouldn't *surprise* us, but it also shouldn't *scare* us. When it comes to our enemy, he is already defeated. Satan was defeated when Christ was resurrected. Christ's resurrection proves that for believers, death doesn't get the final say. Jesus does. The devil's power is limited, and his reign is restricted. Fear tactics are all the enemy has, and his strategies are not rooted in anything absolute or everlasting. When we choose to stand firm because of our confidence in God, it points to the future failure of evil and God's prevailing victory through Jesus.

1:29-30 None of us would sign ourselves up for suffering. But Paul is reminding us that suffering is something that happens *for* us. There are few teachers that are as powerful as suffering when it comes to our spiritual growth. Suffering: 1) allows you to identify with your Savior and the suffering He endured on your behalf; 2) reminds you that this world isn't all there is; 3) serves as an example to others when you endure, as Paul did for the Philippians. Ask God to help you see your suffering as He does.

Philippians 1:12-30

QUESTIONS

Icebreaker: Have you ever been through a difficult situation that God ended up using for good in the long run? Tell us about it.

1. Read Philippians 1:12-13. Go around the circle and let each woman personalize Paul's words for herself with something she's going through that she is confident God will use for His glory: "my _____ is for Christ." Write down everyone's answer and throughout this study, pray for one another specifically.

2. What does Paul's response teach us about how we should deal with those who preach the gospel or share about Jesus with impure motives? Have you ever experienced God working through someone who appeared to have wrong motives? If so, what did you learn from that encounter?

3. In the commentary note on Philippians 1:19, it says: "*Prayer does not change God's plans... However, our prayers are certainly part of God's plan.*" Re-read Philippians 1:19 and discuss what this verse reveals about our prayers. If you're willing to be vulnerable, share if you feel your prayer life reflects the truth in this verse.

4. Philippians 1:19-25 shares Paul's perspective on life and death. What stands out to you from these verses? How do you think Paul's view on life and death is different from most people today? What convictions and circumstances do you think shaped Paul to see both life and death the way he did? How do you view life and death?

5. In Philippians 1:26, Paul combines "*progress and joy in the faith.*" As it says in the commentary: It shouldn't be possible to grow in Jesus and get grumpy. Doesn't this mean that all genuine spiritual progress should also increase our joy?

Practically, what do you think it looks like to progress in our faith and increase in joy simultaneously?

6. Read Philippians 1:27 as a group. Do you think believers take the call to stand *"firm in one spirit, with one mind striving side by side for the faith of the gospel"* seriously? Have a group member read John 17:20-21 aloud. What do Jesus' words remind us of what our unity shows to the world? What are some ways believers could improve our unity with one another?

7. Philippians 1:28-30 reminds us how our faith can impact how we face both opposition and suffering. Share the reminder from these verses or the commentary that you needed most with the group.

🐝 Break into prayer partners and specifically lift one another up using your personalizations of Philippians 1:13.

Philippians 2:1-11

COMMENTARY

2:1-11   Some scholars believe that Paul's words in these verses may have been rooted in an early hymn of the faith. Others believe these are Paul's original words. It would be interesting to know which view is true, for sure, but what's more valuable is meditating on these words and aiming to live more and more in the way that Jesus lived. Pray these words over your walk with Christ, your marriage, your parenting, your pastors and church leaders, your discipleship relationships, your co-workers, your interactions with unbelievers, etc. Read through the gospel accounts in Scripture and really examine the life of Jesus. With every story you read, ask: **What does Christ's example teach me about how I should live?**

2:1   It helps me to take these phrases and turn them into questions to truly reflect on the meaning of each: *Are you encouraged by what Christ has done? Are you comforted by God's love? Do you recognize the participation of the Holy Spirit in you and around you? Have you experienced God's affection and mercy?* (P.S. I pray you shouted "yes!" internally as you read each of those!) Before Paul gives them further instruction, he reminds them of the foundation for his next instruction. All we do as believers is rooted in what has been done for us. There's nothing God calls you to do that He has not done for you first.

2:2   Consider those first three words: *"Complete my joy."* Paul's words remind us that unity with other believers is a critical component to experiencing the complete joy available to us through Jesus. God created us to function as a unit – not merely as individuals. You will not experience God's complete joy in isolation or in division. Constantly come back to the main thing: God's mission matters most, and His love serves as both the authority and the fuel for our unity with one another. Care about what God cares about – and let everything else go.

2:3   Don't simply examine your actions. Pray God will expose your motives. Fiercely pray against your own selfishness and pride, which is the root of much of our sin. You will either serve self or your Savior. Beg for God to help you see others and treat others as more important than yourself. I do want to be clear here, though, because we tend to tiptoe around ambition in Christian circles. The Christian life is not meant to be lived void of ambition. Living your life in a way that aims to live and love as Jesus did will absolutely require your ambition. Be ambitious in loving the Lord and loving others. Recognize that you'll actually find more joy if you aim for the back of the line instead of the front. Selfishness ruins, and humility builds. Honestly, humility and ambition are not talked about enough together, but in the pursuit of being more like Jesus, both should be present. Here are a few other common misconceptions about humility:

1.   Humility is not weakness. *(It's often easier to power up in your own strength. Relying on God's power requires more courage.)*

2.   In the absence of pursuing humility, pride is present. *(There is simply no in between. Without the intentional pursuit of humility, pride takes over.)*

3.   Humility invites God and others in. *(Your pride will shut God and others out.)*

4.   Humility is the path to wisdom. *(Pride may lead to knowledge, but knowledge does not always equal wisdom.)*

2:4   Fun fact from the original Greek: what we translate to be *"interests"* is really a filler word, so Paul's letter was actually very open-ended here. Most clearly, his words here read: *"Let each of you not only look to your own _____, but to the _____ of others."* That leaves this meaning and application to range from topics as weighty as not only looking to your own finances, family, health, and happiness, as well as the daily and mundane moments, not looking only to your own work schedule, weekend plans, restaurant preference or choice of car temperature. It's natural to look after your own interests; God calls us to care about the interests of others just as much. What's rare, goes against our flesh, and what we need to be reminded of is that we're to have the same level of care for others as we naturally have for ourselves. If you know this is an area where you have room for growth, here's a simple evaluation question to pray over: What area of your life are you most consumed by your own interests/desires/needs/wants? This is most likely the area of your life where you will act selfishly instead of selflessly. Surrender this area specifically to the Lord, ask Him to continuously give you opportunities to act on someone else's behalf instead of your own, and beg the Holy Spirit to give you the courage you need to respond in obedience.

2:5   Consider the huge implications of responding in obedience to the last three verses: pursue unity with all believers, refuse to act on your pride and selfish ambition, count others as more significant than yourself, and equate the concerns of others with your personal concerns. Rest in the truth Paul brings us back to here: you don't have to do this on your own. Living the Christian life is not one of willpower, but of God's power. In total transparency, I lived many years trying to live in perfect obedience in my own power. Not only was I unsuccessful, but I was exhausted and super discouraged. Be honest with yourself: who are you relying on – yourself or the Lord? Whose mind do you rely on – yours or Christ's? As His child, you are no longer limited to what you are able to accomplish in your own strength, but what He can do through you. You get to choose your attitude. Lay down your own thoughts, and choose to adopt His.

2:6   Jesus' life didn't begin in Bethlehem; Jesus was with God from the beginning *(See John 1:1-4 for more.)* All three members that make up the Trinity [God the Father, Jesus the Son and the Holy Spirit] are equally God. No member is less God than another. What Paul reminds us of here is that even though Jesus *was* God, He didn't grasp on to what would have benefitted Him the most, but held tightly to the will of His Father. If you and I are honest, though we are *not* God, our flesh constantly prompts the desire to be equal with God. It happened first in the Garden of Eden when the serpent was able to tempt Eve to eat from the one tree God had forbidden so she could be *"like God"* (Genesis 3:4). Although we know how that turned out for Adam and Eve, we continue to grasp on to our desire to be in control. If we were having coffee right now, I would put my drink down and look you in the eyes and remind you of this: There is an enormous gap between the desire to be God and the desire to be *like* Jesus. If Jesus, who was actually God, didn't grasp on to equal status with God, we must put an end to grasping onto anything other than following Jesus' example.

2:7 This does not imply that Jesus ever ceased to be God. However, He willingly gave up all of His "rights" as God to operate within human limits, so that He could 1) be the atonement *(which means the payment that satisfies)* for all sin and 2) give us a perfect example of what a human life lived for God looks like. Jesus chose to serve us instead of holding onto His rights. You simply cannot serve God and others if you're too busy holding on to your rights. Though this is not an exhaustive list, here are a few of the rights we need to lay down in order to live like Jesus so we can serve God and others:

1. The right to our own desires and plans, submitting to God's will instead.

2. The right to control and possess material possessions, instead using them to serve God and others.

3. The right to seek personal recognition and glory, instead giving credit and honor to God.

4. The right to hold grudges and seek revenge, instead practicing forgiveness and exhibiting love and compassion.

5. The right to judge and criticize others, instead extending grace and showing kindness.

2:8 Jesus' obedience to God had no limits. It would have been a downgrade to simply agree to leave Heaven and come to earth, but Jesus humbled Himself as low as He possibly could – death by crucifixion. Not only was crucifixion the most agonizingly painful way to die, it was also the most humiliating death Rome had to offer. From the simple things to genuine matters of life and death, following Jesus' example means our obedience to God shouldn't have limits. Full obedience is not conditional. It's not concerned with comfort or convenience. Ask God to examine your heart and reveal any limits you've put on your obedience so you can fully obey Him.

2:9   This verse reminds us that Jesus humbled Himself, and God
exalted Him. We have an enemy who is crafty, but truthfully, he's
not all that creative. Satan uses the same tricks and traps over
and over – one being that he will consistently tempt you to exalt
yourself instead of humbling yourself as Jesus did. Think about
it: how often do you have the opportunity to elevate your own
importance over God's agenda or the needs of others? Multiple
times every day, right? When you exalt yourself, Scripture tells us
that God will humble you. But if you choose to humble yourself,
you position yourself for God to exalt you *(See Matthew 23:12)*.
Though God's *"exalting"* won't come on our terms or timeline,
we know one day, if we have chosen faith in Christ, God will
grant us eternity in Heaven – which is exaltation none of us
deserve, and yet, God graciously offered it to us through His
Son. *[More on this coming soon! If you want to jump ahead, go
ahead and review the commentary note on Philippians 3:9]*.

2:10-11 Today's world has plenty of people who question who Jesus
was. Many actively deny Him. A day is coming, though, where
no one will wonder any longer. Heaven, earth, and hell will
all bow before Him and confess Jesus is Lord. This is why the
most important decision every person will make is what they
believe about Jesus. How we answer this question determines
where we will spend eternity. As followers of Christ, these verses
should give you confident hope in who Jesus is along with an
extraordinary burden for those who do not know Christ. If you
do not already know the Lord and you're reading this because
you're searching for answers: Jeremiah 29:13 says, *"You will
seek Me and find Me, when you seek me with all your heart."* I
wholeheartedly believe that if you will ask God to reveal Himself
to you and trust that He will, this verse provides the assurance
that this is a prayer God answers the same way 100% of the time.
Jesus is the answer you're searching for. Believe in Him. Jesus is
who He says He is.

Philippians 2:1-11

QUESTIONS

Icebreaker: Humility is a concept that is hard to describe, but impossible to forget when you see it. Have you ever seen someone act with such humility that it's forever ingrained in your mind? Share your story with the group.

1. Before we dig into Paul's instruction, Philippians 2:1 reminds us that everything we do, God has done for us first. How does that help you get the perspective you need to pursue the humility and unity Paul instructs us to have next? Spend some time reminding one another of God's goodness to you by answering these questions:

   - *What are some ways you're encouraged by what Christ has done?*
   - *How does God's love bring you comfort?*
   - *How do you see the Holy Spirit participating in you and around you?*
   - *What are some ways you have experienced God's affection and mercy?*

2. Read Philippians 2:2. What are the things Paul says the Philippians can do to complete his joy? In order to have the kind of unity that Paul instructs here, what are some behaviors and beliefs that disrupt that unity? What are some behaviors and beliefs that build this kind of unity?

3. The commentary note on Philippians 2:3 provides some common misconceptions about humility. Discuss each of them as a group. After you discuss what humility is not, what are some practical ways we can pursue the kind of humility Christ's example calls us to?

4. Philippians 2:5 should fill you with gratitude and hope. You are not asked to live congruent with Jesus' example outside of Jesus' power. Why do we even attempt to live the Christian life in our own strength? What are the practical differences between living in God's power vs. living in your own?

5. Read Philippians 2:6. *(If your group has people with multiple translations of Scripture, this may be a verse that's worth it to read a few times in different ways!)* How much does it humble you to realize that though Jesus was God, He never sought to be equal with God? What are some ways you think we as humans battle trying to be equal with God? What can we learn from Christ's example instead?

6. Philippians 2:7 implies that Jesus gave up all of His "rights" as God to fully obey God and to serve us. The commentary note on 2:7 lists a few rights we need to lay down to follow in Christ's example. Did any of those stand out to you? What other rights would you add to this list?

7. Read Philippians 2:8-11. Jesus' obedience had no limits, and look what God was able to do. Do you think you ever put limitations on your obedience to God? If you're aiming to live as Jesus did, what do you think the cost is whenever we live with limited obedience? How do these verses show us that God responds when we humbly submit to His will? What thoughts come to your mind when you picture the day that everyone will confess that Jesus is Lord?

Philippians 2:12-30

COMMENTARY

2:12   ***"Therefore:"*** As a teenager, I was taught to ask, *"What's 'therefore' there for?"* whenever *therefore* appears in Scripture, and I've never forgotten it. In this case, *therefore* reminds us of the words we studied at the beginning of Philippians 2. Paul's next instruction is possible because of what Jesus has done for us. When we read his words through that lens vs. isolated instruction, it reminds us everything God asks of us is how we are to respond to what Jesus has done for us.

"my beloved, as you have always obeyed, so now, not only as in my presence but much more in my absence:" Paul affirms the way the Philippians have obeyed in the past, and he confirms that continued obedience is critical for their faith to continue to grow. We never move beyond obedience.

"work out your own salvation:" This is the key difference: we work **out** our salvation, we don't work **for** our salvation. It was Jesus' work on the cross that makes salvation possible – not anything you or I can do. In his letter to Ephesus, Paul put it this way: *"For by grace you have been saved through faith. And this is not your own doing; it is the gift of God, not a result of works, so that no one may boast"* (Ephesians 2:8-9). It's worth saying again: we do not work *for* our salvation, but we are to work *out* our salvation. Simply put, Paul is reminding us that we cannot rely on past obedience to continue to grow our faith. We must keep taking faith steps. We must continue living in simple obedience to the Lord. We must keep trusting Him, refusing to lean on our own understanding but choosing to acknowledge Him in all we do. [See Proverbs 3:5-6.]

"with fear and trembling:" This is not a call to obey God because you're scared of Him, but to rightly respond in obedience to His holiness. There are two extremes that are easy to gravitate toward in terms of God's holiness:

1. Realizing God's vastness, greatness and splendor to the point where you question whether or not you really can have a personal relationship with Him.

2. Dismissing God's holiness, attempting to humanize Him to only be slightly bigger than you are – which makes a personal relationship with God seem much more possible, but drastically limits your worship in the absence of recognizing how infinitely much greater God is than you are.

But here's the truth in the tension: God is both powerful enough to create the whole world in mere days, and He's also close enough to be with you as you read these words right now. As part of working out your salvation, ask God to help you see the connection between His holiness and the hope you have in Jesus. God's holiness is why we can have confident hope in Christ – because nothing is impossible for Him. [See Luke 1:37.]

Three quick reflection questions:

1. How has your realization of what Jesus has done for you prompted you to respond recently?

2. What steps are you currently taking for no reason other than faith?

3. How does your view of God's holiness shape your confidence in Christ?

2:13 These words provide even more understanding to the previous verse. **You can work out your salvation because God is working *in* you.** How good is our God that He doesn't even ask us to work out our own salvation with fear and trembling without Him? Not only that, but God supplies us with the desire (*"to will"*) and the power (*"to work"*) to live as He commands. He is both the motivation and the power to act. God works, and so do we – not merely one or the other. Avoid the spiritual ditches that emphasize one over the other.

1. You do not have to attempt working out your salvation in your own power. God's work in the world is the same power that is able to work in you – if you're willing to let Him. God's work in your life is undeniably the Lord and looks nothing like what you can accomplish on your own. Depend on Him – not yourself.

2. God's working in you gives you working *out* your salvation *more* meaning – not less. Yes, God is sovereign. [See Luke 19:38-40]. But God's work in the world doesn't give us permission to be inactive. In the very beginning, God involved us in His work in the world *(Genesis 1:26-27)*. Jesus reaffirmed our involvement in God's work in the world as the conclusion to His earthly ministry *(Matthew 28:19-20)*. Nothing about the Christian life is a call to passivity.

"for His good pleasure:" These are my favorite four words of this verse because they reveal so much about God's character. God's continuous work in you that He is always faithful to complete *(refer back to Philippians 1:6)* is not in any way reluctant, resentful, laborious, or inconvenient. He works in you, not simply because He has work to do, but because as your Heavenly Father, it gives Him great pleasure. The joy we have in doing God's work in the world is yet another reflection of our Father's joy to work in us. God initiates joy with us.

2:14 This is an easy verse to understand, but extremely difficult in application. In clarifying *"all things,"* Paul is reminding us that we are to be obedient to what God says in everything we do. If we are focused on our obedience, we shouldn't have energy leftover to grumble or dispute — with God or others. In this letter, Paul has already given us an example of what this looks like. He would have had seemingly Biblical grounds to oppose those who were teaching the gospel for the wrong reasons, but instead, Paul chose to rejoice instead that the gospel was being preached instead of grumbling or disputing over their motives. [See note on Philippians 1:15-18.] Paul did not question God over why he was in prison while those with wrong motives were free to preach *(and just free in general!)* or complain about or argue with those who attempted to use the gospel for their own gain. Is complaining or arguing getting in the way of you doing all God asks you to do? Lay the complaints and arguments down – no matter how valid they may be – and simply obey God. Complaining rarely causes change, and arguments rarely change minds, let alone hearts.

2:15 Regardless of whether you're naturally feisty or naturally timid, here's your motivation: we refuse to complain and argue so we can shine as lights in the world. Paul is pointing back to words Jesus said: *" You are the light of the world. A city set on a hill cannot be hidden. Nor do people light a lamp and put it under a basket, but on a stand, and it gives light to all in the house.*

In the same way, let your light shine before others, so that they may see your good works and give glory to your Father who is in heaven" (Matthew 5:14-16). As a Christian, it's not a question of *if* you are a light for Christ - you are. But how brightly does your light shine? Paul challenges us to realize that refusing to grumble and complain, especially in situations where grumbling and complaining are justifiable, is another way that our light can shine brightly. In the moments when you're tempted to grumble and dispute, ask yourself: **Is this complaint or argument worth dimming my light?** The darkness of this world is desperate for light. And just like a flicker of light in the midst of darkness can bring hope, comfort and guidance, that's the same opportunity we, as believers, have in the midst of a lost world.

2:16   We usually think of Paul as a prisoner who was bold for the gospel in his chains or the G.O.A.T. [greatest of all time] in terms of missionaries, but this verse really shows Paul's heart as a pastor. He really loved his people. Paul wasn't merely concerned with finishing well in the faith himself. Part of how he endured with joy was on the day when he finally stood before the Lord, he wanted the Philippians to be there with him. He would be confident he did not *"run in vain or labor in vain"* if the Philppians held fast to the gospel along with him. Joyful endurance is not just about your discipline to finish faithfully yourself – but whose faithful finish are you committed to? Joyfully endure *with* others – and their endurance will build your confidence that nothing done for the Lord is wasted *(See 1 Corinthians 15:58).*

2:17-18 In Jewish culture, as well as many other religions during that time, it was customary to add a drink offering to the animal you sacrificed. *[See Numbers 15:4-5 for an Old Testament reference.]* The drink offering involved pouring wine on the altar as an additional offering to the animal you sacrificed. Most of the time, sacrifice is talked about as something we are called to give up. Paul's words here apply the gospel to the normal narrative of sacrifice, challenging both himself and the Philippians to recognize that our greatest potential for joy that lasts isn't something we get, but the sacrifices we make for the sake of the gospel. Essentially, Paul says, *"Don't hold back anything from the Lord. Hand every inch of your life over to Him. Let Him pour you out. Being willing to let God use me in whatever way He sees fit is the greatest joy of my life, and I don't want you to miss it."* Jesus, our ultimate example, fulfilled His life's purpose through sacrifice. As you follow in His example, don't expect fulfillment will come through gain. Be a living sacrifice, and let God fill you with the kind of joy only He can provide.

2:19 Paul wasn't relying on new circumstances to send Timothy to Philippi; he relied on the Lord. Relying on God requires that we trust His way and His timing. Paul's words here also emphasize the importance of gospel community. Paul had everything he needed in Christ alone, but yet, he recognized how encouraged he would be when Timothy came back with a report of all God was doing through the Philippians. Encouragement literally means *"to put courage in."* Encouragement is not merely affirmation. As believers, encouragement is rooted in sharing with one another how we see God moving in our own lives and each other's lives. Don't settle for words of affirmation; put courage in others by pointing out where God is working.

2:20-21 Even among believers, Paul acknowledged that it's hard to find someone who isn't preoccupied with their own life. Don't miss this, though, because this is so much more than us being aware of the needs of others. Paul notes, *"they all seek after their own interests, not those of Christ Jesus."* Go back and review Philippians 2:4. Genuinely caring for others is what Christ did for us, so we do so, not merely for one another, but to follow Jesus' example. Ask God to search your heart on this: are you seeking after your own interests or His?

2:22 I love picturing Paul and Timothy ministering side-by-side. While selfish ambition is not new, it's easier than ever to attempt to do "ministry" alone. While there may be a few times you have to stand alone on the rare Mount Carmels that occur in your life *[See the story of Elijah in 1 Kings 18:20-46]*, there are far more examples in Scripture of men and women partnering together for the furtherance of the gospel. Not to mention, the first problem God realized that existed in the perfect world He created was that Adam was alone, and He solved it by creating Eve. *(See Genesis 2:18).* So in terms of your ministry, who is serving with you? Be intentional to further the gospel alongside other believers.

2:23-24 Obviously, Paul wasn't in control of when he would be released from prison. We don't know all of the details here, but we know that though Timothy was valuable to Paul during this imprisonment, Paul was still more concerned for the Philippians than he was for himself. He trusted the Lord that he would be able to come to them himself eventually, but he didn't want to wait to send Timothy until he would be able to come with him.

2:25   Epaphroditus is from the church at Philippi – the one they sent to deliver money to Paul in prison. Look at the words Paul uses to describe him – *"my brother, fellow worker, fellow soldier, your messenger and minister to my need."* Paul demonstrates his heart behind the words he wrote in 1 Corinthians 12 about how all members of the body are equal in importance. No part is more significant than another. Ephaphroditus' task of delivering money *(and probably a hug!)* to Paul was every bit as much ministry as Paul's letter he wrote back to the Philippians. Transparently, can I just ask you: are you as exhausted as I am that we tend to make hierarchies of gifts and places of service in the church? Let's stop assigning ranks to certain gifts. Let's stop putting anyone on a pedestal other than Jesus. Every believer is your brother/sister, your fellow worker, your fellow soldier, your messenger and minister. God is big enough to use each of us this way. Let's live like we believe that's exactly what God is doing.

2:26-28   Along the journey, Epaphroditus became very ill – and nearly died. Paul's words indicate that perhaps the plan was for Epaphroditus to stay longer with Paul, beyond merely delivering the money. But because of what he had been through, Epaphroditus longed to be back home with his church family. Paul is so grateful that Epaphroditus lived, he is more than happy to send him back home alive. His death would have been much more tragic than Paul missing him when he went back to Philippi. I love that Paul acknowledges how God had mercy on both Epaphroditus *and* himself. Again, he gives us insight into what loving others through the love of Christ looks like. When you see God move in the life of someone you love, the mercy they experience from God is a fresh wave of His mercy on your life too. Limiting your love for others limits the goodness of God you'll get to experience.

2:29-30   Paul wants to ensure they recognize God is the One who allowed Epaphroditus to come back to them. He also encourages them to honor Epaphroditus for risking his life to do the work of Christ. On a large scale, we should honor the brave men and women who serve as missionaries around the world. Pray for the believers in countries where worship services have to take place underground because worshipping God isn't allowed. Thank God for them. It's also worth considering how to apply this on a smaller scale too. Paul encourages the Philippians to honor those who complete *"what was lacking in your service…"* Think about all the areas, just in your church, where you don't serve. Honor those who serve where you cannot. We need one another.

Philippians 2:12-30

QUESTIONS

Icebreaker: Tell us about someone who worked with you repeatedly to teach you how to do something. What did they teach you to do, and how long did it take you to learn?

1. In Philippians 2:12, the connecting word *"therefore"* reminds us that everything we studied in Philippians 2:1-11 is the foundation for obeying the instruction that follows. How does it change your perspective to consider that your obedience to these words is merely your response to what Jesus has done for you? Practically, how do you keep Jesus' example as your aim?

2. Read Philippians 2:12-13. Discuss the difference between working for your salvation vs. working out your salvation. Which extreme would you fall into most easily – living as if you have to earn your salvation or living spiritually inactive since God is sovereign? In what ways can you ensure you live in a way that works *out* your salvation while God works *in* you?

3. In light of Philippians 2:14-15, have you ever considered how complaining and arguing get in the way of our ability to obey? Do you think most of the complaints and arguments Christians engage in are worth dimming our lights to the lost world? How can we hold one another accountable to look different from the world in this way?

4. In Philippians 2:16-18, Paul paints a picture of how he will know every sacrifice he made was worth it when he stands before the Lord and the Philippians are there with him. How does picturing others there with us before Jesus impact how we see the sacrifices we make now? Who do you picture with you? How does picturing them standing before the Lord give you joyful endurance to finish faithfully – even when your circumstances are difficult?

5. Read Philippians 2:20-21 where Paul talks about why he hopes to send Timothy to Philippi soon. Practically, what do you think it looks like to live in a way that seeks after Christ's interests? What does it look like to seek your own interests? What are some indicators you've learned to recognize when you're living in a way that seeks your own interests instead of Christ's? In Philippians 2:19-25, Paul shares how Timothy and Epaphroditus followed the example Jesus set for us. What stood out to you about each of these men – both their actions and the way Paul spoke about them in these verses?

6. In Philippians 2:29-30, Paul challenges the Philippians to honor those who serve the Lord in ways that we do not. How can you protect yourself from your pride and intentionally honor, pray for and be grateful for those who are standing in different gospel gaps than you are? Share one action step you'll take this week to encourage (*put courage in!*) another believer.

Philippians 3:1-11

3:1   It matters that Paul writes, *"rejoice **in** the Lord."* So many times, we settle for rejoicing in our circumstances. While some circumstances will cause you to rejoice, you will also experience trials. [See James 1:2-4.] You will endure suffering. [See Romans 5:3-5.] You will face persecution. [See 2 Timothy 3:12.] But through every circumstance, good or bad, you will always have reason to rejoice **in** Jesus. The real question is: *do you remember what Jesus has done for you so you will rejoice, or do you often forget about Him?* Remember Jesus so you will rejoice.

Paul has already referenced the importance of rejoicing several times in his letter; so here, he acknowledges that he knows he's repeating himself. But note what he says about his repetition:

1. ***"To write the same things to you is no trouble to me:"*** If you're in the trenches of discipleship, you *should* feel like you repeat yourself all the time. It's not just you. All of Scripture points to Jesus. Many different stories are told, but the entire Bible foreshadows, tells and echoes back to the one story of how our loving and One True God went to great lengths to save His people through His Son. Do not get frustrated or discouraged – *with yourself or with others* – when you repeat yourself. Have the mindset that it's no trouble.

2. ***"and is safe for you:"*** The further away we get from the foundational truth of the gospel, the more dangerous the message is for our hearers. Dangerous is not too strong of a word; **distraction is dangerous.** A life truly lived for Christ is not a life of merely sin avoidance, but requires us to actively follow Jesus' example. Living distracted can have every bit of the same effect as living idle. By repeating foundational gospel principles, like rejoicing in the Lord, you are limiting distractions for yourself and those around you, and in doing so, keeping all of you safe through remaining focused on the main mission.

3:2-3   Here, Paul warns the Philippians of the evil they can expect to encounter inside the church – not just outside of it. This is actually a really powerful word picture. By Paul telling the Philippians to look out for the *"dogs," "the evildoers"* and *"those who mutilate the flesh,"* Paul is reducing circumcision, a sign of the covenant God made with Abraham [see Genesis 17:9-14] to mutilating the flesh – *if* the act of circumcision puts your confidence in what you have done instead of what Jesus has done. While we may not consider the spiritual reasons for circumcision very much now, this problem still exists: obedience outside of the transforming power of Jesus is merely behavior management. Behavior management is all about you – your ability to control your sin and do good works, your willpower, and your image. Behavior management requires you to do every right action in your own strength. God changing your heart becomes an afterthought, at best. If you've never been there, take it from me: it's absolutely exhausting. Living in behavior modification mode leaves you to confront all of the same problems, such as your flesh and the broken world, without the realities that the gospel makes possible – such as Jesus' righteousness being added to your account and the power of the Holy Spirit dwelling in you. Paul's caution goes beyond looking out for others who are living this way; he is warning them to avoid getting caught up in behavior modification instead of gospel transformation themselves. Do not merely conform to a set of behaviors, a religion, or a morality compass. Let Jesus capture your heart and change your life. Let the gospel truly transform you from the inside out. Don't settle for behavior modification. Put your confidence in Christ and what He has done – not in what you can do.

View the chart on the next page to help
you discern the difference:

BEHAVIOR MODIFICATION	GOSPEL TRANSFORMATION
☐ Emphasis on what I do/don't do	☐ Emphasis on what Jesus has done/ will do
☐ Goal is to be better	☐ Goal is to be more like Jesus
☐ Do right out of obligation	☐ Do right out of love
☐ Sin —> Shame	☐ Sin —> Repentance
☐ Relies on my willpower	☐ Relies on Christ's power
☐ Image-Keeper (identity in self)	☐ Image-Bearer (identity in Christ)
☐ Rooted in rules	☐ Rooted in love
☐ Mission is self-focused	☐ Mission is others-focused
☐ Hopes in what the world can offer me now	☐ Hopes for what Jesus has made possible for me in heaven
☐ Joy based on how good I am	☐ Joy based on how good God is

3:4-6   Paul does not list his credentials here out of arrogance, but to make a point to those who are consumed with or confused by legalism. In order to strengthen his argument, Paul shares all of the things he could rely on instead of Jesus, but does not. Again, Paul doesn't lay his spiritual resumé out to boast, but to point out that if anyone would be pleasing the Lord because of merely being good at being good, Paul would be at the top of the list – not any of them. Compared to every other qualifier, Paul would have been more accomplished.

Here's the unspoken meaning behind Paul's list:

"circumcised on the eighth day:" —> I've kept the rules from the very beginning of my life.

"of the nation of Israel:" —> I'm part of God's original chosen people.

48

"of the tribe of Benjamin:" —> Many key people of faith are my ancestors.

"a Hebrew born of Hebrews:" —> When others caved to the Greek culture around us, my family and I remained strong in all of the beliefs and practices of the Jewish faith.

"regarding the law, a Pharisee:" —> I am an expert in the law, and many consider me to be spiritually elite. Most can't be a Pharisee because they're unable to memorize as much Scripture and study as much is required – but I did.

"regarding zeal, persecuting the church:" —> Before I came to faith in Christ, I was so passionate about protecting Jewish tradition that I was able to instill fear in every person who followed Jesus. I was even able to convince the government to support my persecution efforts!

"regarding the righteousness that is in the law, blameless:" —> Pick any random rule in Leviticus you want. Not only do I know each of them from memory, but you won't be able to find a single rule I haven't kept.

3:7   Paul no longer puts his confidence in himself to prove his righteousness. Christ's work on the cross and resurrection changes everything, and yet, it's all too easy to fall into belief and behavior patterns that put more hope in merely legalism or moralism instead of what Jesus did for us. The gospel makes possible what religion cannot, which is why Paul says all of his good religious activity of the past is a loss to him.

Paul's words here also serve as our reminder of the two ditches outside of the gospel to avoid:

Works-Based Salvation: Every command God gives and boundary He sets is for your flourishing. While you have far more to gain from obedience than disobedience, Jesus' death on the cross, that served as the payment for your sins, proves that your obedience doesn't *earn* you any of the grace God has shown you. *That* is the difference: Jesus earned your righteousness before God; you did not. In two of his other letters, Paul communicates a similar message this way:

"For the wages of sin is death, but the gift of God is eternal life in Christ Jesus our Lord." - Romans 6:23

"For you are saved by grace through faith, and this is not from yourselves; it is God's gift— not from works, so that no one can boast." - Ephesians 2:8-9

Cheap Grace: "Cheap grace" is a term originally coined and thoroughly explained by Deitrich Bonhoeffer in his book, *The Cost of Discipleship*. Far less eloquently put than he said it, cheap grace is the belief that you can somehow take advantage of the fact that Jesus already paid for your sin and so you choose to live however you want. This belief ignores the real cost of Jesus' sacrifice and the weight of our sin before a holy God. God's grace and mercy does not make sin safe or make Jesus' sacrifice trivial.

Here are a few verses to meditate on through this lens:

"Let not sin therefore reign in your mortal body, to make you obey its passions. Do not present your members to sin as instruments for unrighteousness, but present yourselves to God as those who have been brought from death to life, and your members to God as instruments for righteousness. For sin will have no dominion over you, since you are not under law but under grace." - Romans 6:12-14

"He himself bore our sins in his body on the tree, that we might die to sin and live to righteousness. By his wounds you have been healed." - 1 Peter 2:24

We are saved by grace, and we continue to be sanctified in grace for all of our earthly lives. The gospel saves us, and the gospel sustains us. Your faith is far more about what has been done for you than it will ever be about what you have done. This should fill your life with wondrous worship, which will supply all the zeal you need to follow Him as closely as you can.

3:8   In case the Philippians glossed over his previous statement or somehow minimized it, Paul repeats himself in a way that uses stronger language that accurately conveys his deep conviction. As long as he has Jesus, Paul can lose anything else. Referring back to the elaborate resumé he laid out in verses 5-6, Paul is adamant that knowing Jesus is infinitely better. Knowing Jesus puts everything else in its proper place. Part of gaining Christ is losing whatever we cling to instead of Him. Following Jesus means that He is truly the Lord of your life. Lordship means Jesus is in charge, not you. His way is the right way. Attempting to live for Jesus in a way that needs Jesus *and* anything else to be satisfied *isn't* fully living for Jesus. Good or bad, whatever you hold onto that isn't Jesus is holding you back from the freedom and fullness only He can offer you. Maybe your past history looks similar to Paul's. You were raised in the church and you've done pretty well on the list of do's and don'ts. There's nothing wrong with that being your story – as long as you don't rely on it. Or maybe you're reading this, and you're feeling the complete opposite: you feel like you don't have a resumé to rely on at all. That's okay too: you don't need one.

3:9   Jesus is your resumé now. In one of his sermons on this text, Charles Spurgeon pointed out how Paul renounces his own righteousness as eagerly as most renounce their sins. Instead, we get to grasp the righteousness that Christ made possible for us – that both *comes through* faith and *depends on* faith. Again, faith hinges on what God has done, is doing and will do – not what we have done, are doing or will do. These words are easy to say but cannot be lived outside of faith. The reality of God's grace goes so against our fleshly nature, that truly believing and behaving in a way that mirrors this truth must come from Him and depend on Him.

3:10-11 These two verses articulate the three beliefs that fuel knowing Christ:

1. **Jesus' life + death:** God created a beautiful world. He created man, and He created woman, and it didn't take long for His creation to begin searching for happiness outside of Him. When sin entered the world, it separated us from God, because God is perfectly holy. But praise God, He is also perfectly loving. In His perfect love, in actions that go beyond our understanding, God sent His son, Jesus, to earth to do what we could never do: live

a perfect, sinless life. Jesus' life had one main mission: to die as the sinless sacrifice that our sin requires for us to be reconciled to God. Jesus accomplished God's purpose for His earthly life. In our place, Jesus died by crucifixion and was buried. *(In addition to this being the main story of the Bible, you will not find one secular source that disagrees that Jesus was a man who really lived, really died, and that three days later, His tomb was empty.)*

2. **The power of His resurrection:** Jesus' story on earth doesn't end with death. Three days later, Jesus conquered death – and with it, all of our sin. He rose again. Jesus' death and resurrection is not just a way, but the way to be reconciled with God.

3. **Jesus' coming reign:** After His resurrection, Jesus ascended to the Father in Heaven, and right now, He is waiting for the Father's instruction to come back to earth for those who believe in Him. I know that most Christians feel uncertain or uneasy concerning the end times. I'll be the first to admit: there's plenty in Revelation I don't fully understand, and this side of heaven, I'm not sure I ever will. But here's what I am confident in: the end times shouldn't prompt us to freak out or even attempt to figure out, but instead, they give us hope for what we have in Heaven because of Jesus!

The life you live, you live by faith in His life, His death, His resurrection, and His coming reign. What a Savior!

Philippians 3:1-11

QUESTIONS

Icebreaker: If we were to get a copy of your resumé, what is the most impressive thing and the most embarrassing thing we would find on it?

1. Philippians 3 once again begins with a reminder to rejoice in the Lord. Be honest: do you have trouble remembering to rejoice in Jesus? Practically, what are some rhythms we can incorporate into our regular routine to remember what Jesus has done for us so we can rejoice in Him? Also, what are some unhealthy habits that may prompt us to forget Him so we are left to merely rejoice in our circumstances?

2. Refer back to the chart under the commentary note on Philippians 3:2-3 that distinguishes between behavior modification and gospel transformation. Go through each line as a group, and discuss how to replace the behavior modification with the gospel transformation.

3. In Philippians 3:5-6, Paul lists out his past accomplishments that he once counted as his righteousness. What do you think relying on your own righteousness looks like today? Work together to create a spiritual resumé someone today may attempt to rely on instead of Jesus.

4. Read Philippians 3:7. The commentary note described two ditches we need to avoid on either side of the gospel: works-based salvation and cheap grace. What are some practical ways we can avoid falling into either ditch? *(If you're feeling vulnerable, share which ditch you're most likely to find yourself in if left unchecked.)*

5. Paul's strong language in Philippians 3:8 shares that he looks at what he formerly viewed as righteousness as rubbish in order

to gain Christ. Part of gaining Christ is letting go of anything else we may depend on instead of Him. Is there anything you need to loosen your grip on/let go of so you can experience the fullness and freedom of living in a way that just wants Jesus? [Confession is uncomfortable, but it's the first step to removing the power any idol has over us.]

6. Read Philippians 3:9-11. As a group, discuss the impact each of these truths have on your faith in Christ to remind yourself of the hope offered to us through the gospel: 1) Jesus' life and death; 2) the power of Jesus' resurrection; 3) Jesus' coming reign. Practically, how do we live in a way that trusts in and relies on our faith above anything else?

7. Read Revelation 19:11-16. This is the picture of Jesus you should have as you pray. The first time He came to earth, Jesus came as the Suffering Servant. When He comes back for us *(and He is really coming back!)*, Jesus will come as a Victorious Warrior. How does this picture of Jesus impact your confidence as you pray?

Philippians 3:12-21

COMMENTARY

3:12   When Paul writes he has not already obtained *this*, he's referring to eternal life. Paul marvels that though he will wait for the eternal reward for believing in Jesus – the gift of eternal life, which will allow us to finally be free from the brokenness of the world that sin caused (*"perfect"*) – he can live in the power of Jesus *now* because of what Jesus has done. Note the different tenses of the verbs he uses: *"press on"* is present-tense and in the Greek, indicates a continuous action. *"Has made"* is past tense. In other words, Paul can press into the hope he has in heaven *now* because of what Jesus has *already* done. Jesus gives each of us the same hope. You can keep hoping for heaven, despite the heaviness and brokenness of the world around you, and despite your own sin. In the work Jesus completed on the cross, He made you His own. If you are always attempting to manage your sin or control your outcomes, not only will you be exhausted, but it won't work. The gospel provides you with the power you need to press on and keep pressing. Following Him has you headed in the right direction, even if you aren't there yet. Press on – *and keep pressing* – into Jesus until heaven.

3:13   Don't miss that Paul refers to the Philippians as siblings. The word likely translated *"brothers"* in your Bible is a collective term, more accurately indicating *"brothers and sisters,"* since Paul's letter was to the men, women and children of the church at Philippi. When it comes to how we view other believers, our most accurate perception of one another is that of spiritual siblings. Think practically about this for a moment: how do earthly siblings behave? They disagree and get on one another's nerves. They're there for one another during life's highs and lows. Even if they're mad at each other, they often find themselves sharing a dinner table, the backseat of a car, or a roof over their heads. They are also highly protective of one another. While they each have particular traits and behaviors

55

that drive the other crazy, if anyone else dares to say a negative word, siblings will typically stand up to defend one another. *That's* the kind of relationship we're supposed to have with one another inside the church. The people we worship God with and serve alongside should be far more like siblings than strangers or mere acquaintances. *[This was not Paul's idea. See Matthew 12:48-50 for Jesus' teaching that our family is defined by whoever does the will of God.]*

Once again, Paul acknowledges that the reward coming to him in heaven has nothing to do with what he has done, but is possible because of what Jesus has done. God's grace is probably one of the hardest things for our flesh to comprehend, because human nature tends to be hard-wired for justice *(at least for others!)* God doesn't love you because you're good, because you earned it, or because you're worthy on your own. He loves you, He sent Jesus to die in your place to earn your right-standing before God – because you're His. He created you. He knit you together in your mother's womb *(Psalm 139:13)*. God made a way for you to be reconciled to Him through Jesus while you were still a sinner *(Romans 5:8)*. On your own, you do not add anything to God's gift of salvation. Humble yourself, and be confident in Christ.

Pressing on indicates you're looking ahead. When it comes to where your focus lies, to press on means to stop looking back and to stop looking around. *"What lies behind"* is not just your past, but everything you're enduring now. It reminds me of the words John wrote in his first letter: *"And the world is passing away along with its desires, but whoever does the will of God abides forever"* (1 John 2:17). This world, everything in it, and all it attempts to offer you, is already passing away. Don't look to the world to solve your problems, to satisfy you or to give you hope. For that, we must look to God and aim at heaven.

3:14   The goal is heaven, and the prize is that one day, we will be face-to-face with Jesus. The good ol' days have not already happened, but there is a good day coming! The joy that Paul has continued to bring up through his letter? *This* is the mindset where that joy comes from. Because of what Jesus has done, because eternal life with Him is a real thing for those who confess Him as Lord, we can have confident joy in what is yet to come! But in order to experience that unshakeable and unwavering joy in the midst of this broken world, we must refuse to dwell on what will one day be behind us – this world. Nothing you're enduring right now will overwhelm you in heaven. Take the peace that Jesus gives *(John 14:27)*, dwell on heaven, and spend your earthly days pressing on in the joyful endurance He makes possible.

3:15   Often, spiritual maturity is wrongly defined by insufficient measurements: Bible knowledge, perfect church attendance, etc. Paul defines spiritual maturity for us very differently. Spiritual maturity is wanting Jesus, not other things. Spiritual maturity is relying on Jesus, not anyone else. Spiritual maturity is hoping in Jesus, not anything else – or even Jesus *and* anything else. Spiritual maturity longs for more of heaven, not more of earth. *This* is the mindset and heart posture of spiritual maturity. How do you get there if you're not there yet? Just like Paul writes: *"God will reveal that also to you."* There's no way to force yourself into it or fake it 'til you make it with spiritual maturity. Pray and ask God to mature your thought life so you can be made more like His Son. Ask Him to align your desires with His desires. When He transforms you by the renewal of your mind *(Romans 12:2)*, you will grow in spiritual maturity because of the work He starts and sustains in you. There are no shortcuts or steps you can take apart from God to become more spiritually mature.

3:16   *Only* hold to the gospel. Hold tightly *only* to what Jesus has done for you. I can speak to this personally: it creates so much tension in your life when you want Jesus *and* anything else. You will be divided if you attempt to live in a way that is amazed by what Jesus has done *and* desires for others to be amazed by what you do. Whenever I've tried to seek the Lord *and anything else*, chaos follows—and quickly. Matthew 6:33 is one to memorize – *"But seek first the kingdom of God and his righteousness, and all these things will be added to you."* You seek God, and He adds everything else. You cling to the truth of what He has done for you, and He'll order the rest. If you add to what you seek or what you white-knuckle, you will only add complication and confusion. Simplify your earthly life by holding fast to the gospel and giving God everything else.

3:17 Paul is not boasting in himself; he is confident that Christ lives in him. There is a distinct difference between the two. He tells the Philippians to imitate him because just as Jesus was our perfect example, we can also encourage one another as we live for Christ. Look to others who have been changed by Jesus and live by His power. Get as close as you can with those who have made the gospel the main mission of their life. No human will ever be a replacement for Jesus' example because Jesus lived a perfect, sinless life, and we are all sinners in need of a Savior. God gave us Jesus as our perfect example, but He chose to give us one another too. The chart below highlights some key Scriptures that detail how we are called to walk in Jesus' example alongside one another:

love one another (JOHN 13:35)	**stir one another up to love and good works** (HEBREWS 10:24-25)
sharpen one another (PROVERBS 27:17)	**bear one another's burdens** (GALATIANS 6:2)
use our gifts to minister to one another (1 PETER 4:10)	**encourage and build one another up** (1 THESSALONIANS 5:11)
confess your sins to one another and pray for each other (JAMES 5:16)	**teach and admonish one another** (COLOSSIANS 3:16)
be hospitable to one another (1 PETER 4:9)	**be unified so the world will believe in Jesus** (JOHN 17:21)

3:18-19 It grieves Paul to have to warn them, once again, about those who have an agenda other than Jesus. Paul alerts them concerning those who *"walk as enemies of the cross of Christ."* By wording it this way, Paul is likely referring to two different groups: those who are vehemently against the gospel as well as those who claim the gospel with their words but live drastically different from the way Jesus did. Specifically, he warns them that:

"their end is destruction:" It may look enticing at times to live the world's way, but choosing to live for yourself instead of for the Lord ends with torment and eternal separation from God. Do not be swayed by instant gratification. Think with eternity in mind.

"their god is their belly:" Those who live for themselves only look out for their own desires. They chase after what they want, unbothered by how their actions affect anyone other than themselves. [Chasing after the world will leave you empty every single time. For a thorough discussion of this in Scripture, consider studying the last words of King Solomon using *Conversational Commentary on Ecclesiastes: Wisdom to Live for Heaven While on Earth.*]

"they glory in their shame, with minds set on earthly things:" Living for yourself is actually worshiping yourself. Whatever glory they attempt to claim for themselves will not last. Along with the earth, it will fade away, and they will be left with nothing.

3:20 Remember, Philippi is a Roman colony, full of Roman patriotism. At the time this was written, Roman citizens were the most elite of the elite. Concluding his discussion on pressing on toward heaven instead of living for earth, Paul urges them in the strongest way he knows how to not get sucked in, no matter how good this world attempts to make it look or how many perks our culture promises. Because we belong to Jesus, our citizenship is already in heaven, even though we're not there yet. Is there a tension in living between the already and not yet? For sure – but note Paul's words: *"from it, we await a Savior, the Lord Jesus Christ."* We serve a God who came *and* is coming back! His return could be *centuries* from now or *seconds* from now. Let's be ready.

3:21 I love the contrast Paul creates using the terms *"lowly body"* for our earthly bodies and *"glorious body"* for our heavenly bodies. Once again, Paul wants us to understand how much this earth and what it has to offer pales in comparison to what God has in store for us in heaven. Don't settle for what the world has to offer you. What is available to us, solely through Christ's power, is worth the wait.

Philippians 3:12-21

QUESTIONS

Icebreaker: Have you ever had to wait on something for so long that you became impatient? Share about how in your impatience, you settled for something less and regretted your choice. Or in contrast, share how by choosing patience, the wait was worth it.

1. Spend a few minutes together as a group dwelling on heaven. What do you think it will be like to see Jesus face-to-face? What other promises do we have in Scripture to let us know how heaven will be different than what we experience on earth?

2. In verses 13 and 17, Paul refers to the church at Philippi as his spiritual siblings. Read Matthew 12:48-50. How did Jesus teach us to define who belongs to our family? Practically, what do you think it looks like to function like brothers and sisters in Christ in the church? Are you currently living like a spiritual sibling with those in your church family? If so, in what ways? If not, what are some steps you could take to have more of a sibling relationship with those you worship God with and serve alongside?

3. In this passage, how does Paul define maturing in our faith? Before studying these verses, how would you have described spiritual maturity? How do we hold ourselves and one another accountable to maturity as these verses define it?

4. Read Philippians 3:17 and review the commentary note on this verse. How do we live in the way God wants us to with one another? How can we be examples for one another without exalting humans over Christ or putting humans on pedestals they don't belong on?

5. Use the following chart to discuss the difference between having an earthly perspective and an eternal perspective. In addition to getting practical with what each viewpoint looks like, confess which area you have the hardest time keeping an eternal perspective.

EARTHLY PERSPECTIVE	ETERNAL PERSPECTIVE
I view my life and what's in it from my perspective.	I view my life and what's in it from God's perspective.
I extend my maximum energy to what appears to matter now.	I extend my maximum energy to what will matter when I stand before the Lord.
The worries of life rule between my heart and my circumstances.	The peace of Christ rules between my heart and my circumstances.

The answers to the final questions will be very personal in nature *(which is okay – because Jesus made it personal when He came down from heaven to make a way for you and for me!)* As for what helps you feel close to the Lord, it may be the ocean for some and mountains for others, or solitude for some and community for others. Similarly, what distracts some *(maybe being too goal-oriented or people pleasing)* may be no problem for others. Different answers are not only allowed – they're expected! Encourage your group members to really reflect on this – in your discussion and after your meeting as well. God made you uniquely, and how He wired you is not an accident.

6. A recurring theme in these verses is to *only* pursue the gospel, to *only* pursue Jesus, and to *only* dwell on heaven. With that in mind, what reminds you of God, makes you feel closer to Jesus, and helps you dwell on heaven? *(Examples – sunsets, the ocean, your child sitting in your lap, deep Bible study on your own or with friends, etc.)*

7. Just like we know what helps us dwell on heaven, we should also know what earthly distractions affect us the most. What distracts you from dwelling on heavenly things? *(Examples – people pleasing, being a good "rule follower," having too many opinions on what others should do, conspiracy theories, competitive work environments, etc.)*

Philippians 4:1-9

COMMENTARY

4:1 Consider each of the ways Paul describes his relationship with the Philippians just in this one verse:

- *"my brothers:"* Refer back to the commentary note on Philippians 3:13 to refresh your memory on what Paul means when he refers to them as spiritual siblings.

- *"whom I love and long for/my beloved:"* Paul's love for the Philippians is not rooted in sentimentality. He cares for them on the deepest level and misses them wholeheartedly.

- *"my joy and crown:"* In the Greek, there are two separate words for the word *"crown:"* one which signifies the crown worn by the king and another to represent crowns that could be earned through achievement. Here, Paul uses the latter. Paul desires for them to know that their willingness to cling to the hope of their salvation and the faith they have in the Lord will be a victory for him that will come with great joy. Remember: It was unpopular to be a Christian in Philippi. If we were to categorize the church at Philippi as an earthly organization, it did not meet the measurements the world would deem as successful. Yet, Paul said their willingness to joyfully endure would be his crowning achievement. As you aim your life to represent Christ, pray for desire that your greatest achievement will involve the enduring faith of someone else.

Paul's charge to *"stand firm"* links back to the hope we have in heaven and the power of Christ's resurrection. (We know this by his use of *"therefore"* to kick off this thought.) Your power to stand firm in the Lord is not limited to your determination or willpower, but the power of Jesus. The proof you can rely on Him for your future is based on what He has already done for you. **Remember it this way: If you can trust God with your eternity, you can trust Him for your right now.**

4:2-3   Standing firm in the Lord creates unity among believers. If His way and His mission are guiding the way, nothing has the power to unite like the gospel. However, these verses call out two women of the church at Philippi *(Euodia and Syntyche)* who are in the middle of a disagreement. We do not know all the details of their argument, but here's what we do know:

- Paul is begging for a resolution of this issue. To **"entreat"** is an earnest request, and Paul makes this ask of both women individually.

- Because Paul asks them to **"agree in the Lord,"** the argument is not over a gospel issue. These women are disagreeing and creating division over something that doesn't matter as much as Jesus.

- When Paul was in Philippi with them, Euodia and Syntyche both served the church alongside him and one another. Paul has seen God work in them and through them with his own eyes. They were leaders, not just in the church, but leaders of the gospel mission in Philippi. Paul asks the whole church, whomever is willing to be their **"true companion,"** to help them reconcile. Though this disagreement was only between these two women, it's likely that the rift between them was also causing problems for others in the church. Frequent advice in the world is not to get in the middle of an argument, but it's different when the argument is disrupting gospel unity. Even though it may be uncomfortable, be willing to be a real friend by helping others resolve issues that are getting in the way of the gospel mission and the unity God calls us to display.

Unfortunately, this is not an isolated event. Division among believers happens far too frequently – and far too easily. Because we live in a world that idolizes our personal opinions, it's extremely countercultural to lay down your opinion for the sake of unity. But because God tells us we will be identifiable as His disciples by our love for one another *(John 13:35)* and our unity will prove that God sent Jesus into the world *(John 17:21)*, we must make unity our priority with other believers. But not just any unity — unity in Jesus. Many Christians today *are* pursuing unity – but they're trying to unify on issues and opinions, not the gospel. Again – nothing unites like the gospel. Pursuing unity on secondary and tertiary issues will NOT create gospel results. Only Jesus can do what Jesus can do. Agreeing on Him has more than enough weight to settle any other disagreement.

4:4   Rejoice always, and say it again…and again… and again. On repeat, as Paul does with this letter, remind yourself to rejoice. If you will make the effort to rejoice because of Jesus – what He has done and what He will do – that one shift really can be the perspective you need to experience the joy that is only available through Him. Joy through Jesus is not altered by your circumstances and does not require anything additional that this world has to offer.

4:5   I love Paul's use of the word **"reasonableness"** here. Jesus left heaven to come to earth, lived the sinless life you never could, died the death you deserved, paid the debt you owed, and defeated death so you can spend eternity with Him, forever reconciled and reunited with your Creator! Rejoicing really is the reasonable response to Jesus. When you find yourself fighting for joy, remind yourself to be reasonable and rejoice!

Also, don't skip over that **"be known to everyone."** Joy – our reasonable response – should be the main emotion that we exude to those around us. This is not referring to forced happiness, but our real response to the one true God. **"The Lord is at hand"** reminds us that beyond living in a way that responds to our circumstances, we get to live joyfully in response to what Jesus has done, is doing, and will do.

4:6   Paul's words here seem to echo the words of Jesus: *"I have told you these things, so that in me you may have peace. In this world you will have trouble. But take heart! I have overcome the world"* (John 16:33). Trouble in the world can absolutely produce some anxiety. But instead of giving into our feelings of anxiousness, Paul gives two alternative directives here.

- **Rejoice > Anxiety.** By reminding us to rejoice and encouraging us to not be anxious, Paul implies that if we focus on rejoicing in Jesus instead of being occupied by the worries of the world, we will automatically have less reason to be anxious. When we hone in on what Jesus is doing in the world instead of dwelling on the trouble of the world, we will expend more energy rejoicing than we will being anxious.

- **Prayer >Anxiety.** Because we will have trouble in the world, there will always be reason to worry. But instead of simply worrying, Paul reminds us to bring our worries to God in prayer. On its own, worry simply produces more anxiety. Prayer can actually yield results. Whatever you're worried about is what you should be praying about. Just in case you're wondering if God cares about what you worry about, note that this verse tells us to pray ***"in everything."*** Nothing in your life is too big or too insignificant to bring to God. He is both big enough to be God and close enough to care about you. Consider this: if you, an imperfect human being, can find it in yourself to care about what your kids/spouse/friends worry about, how much *more* and how much *better* do you think God cares for your worries? While you can't predict what God will do, you can be confident He cares. Bring your worries to God in prayer, and approach Him ***"with thanksgiving"*** – with active gratitude. Praise Him for who He is, what He's done, and how you see Him moving. Praise has a way of activating your faith as you remind yourself of God's faithfulness.

HOW TO REPLACE ANXIETY

REJOICE IN JESUS

TURN WORRIES INTO PRAYERS

PRAISE GOD

4:7 Because we battle our desire for control, instead of seeking God and His presence *(which comes with His peace!)*, we seek answers instead. We wrongly desire more understanding instead of what we really need – more faith. Fellow recovering control-freaks, this would be a good verse to memorize. God's peace is what will guard your heart and your mind – not knowledge. God's peace **"surpasses all understanding"** – meaning His peace is infinitely better than whatever you can figure out. You may not be able to explain the peace in your heart and mind, but you will not be able to deny the peace you experience. I love the imagery the word *"guard"* creates. Picture God as a military presence, protecting your heart and your mind as you come to Him with whatever is making you anxious.

4:8 The human brain truly is magnificent, and God was so good to give us brains so that we would have the ability to reason, to be creative, and to have a "control center" for our bodies – just for starters. However, it is possible for you to feel as if you're being consumed by your thoughts. Maybe you've even battled overthinking – where you dwell on something so much that your thinking is no longer beneficial. It reminds me of something Paul wrote in his second letter to the church at Corinth: *"We demolish arguments and every pretension that sets itself up against the knowledge of God, and we take captive every thought to make it obedient to Christ"* (2 Corinthians 10:6).

As you navigate living for Christ in a broken world, you will encounter circumstances that will easily cause your thoughts to spiral out of control – and fast. Somer Phoebus *(my best friend and ministry partner)* coined the phrase "SPIRAL UP," using this verse as the foundation. Rejoicing in the Lord is the only thing that stands a chance to flip the script in our minds and prayerfully stop intrusive thoughts before they have a chance to form. But in order to do that, we have to think about what we think about – which is what Paul encourages the Philippians to do here.

Think about it this way: there are foods that are rich in nutrients and minerals and nourish your body when you eat them, and there are others foods with little to no nutritional value that can make you feel sluggish and or even sick after you eat them. In a similar way, your thoughts are fuel for your mind. How often

do you take inventory of what's filling your mind? Take out your phone or a sheet of paper, and do a quick brain dump. What thoughts consume your mind? When it gets quiet or you're trying to fall asleep, what do you find yourself thinking about?

Check your brain dump against the list Paul gives us to filter through your thoughts:

"whatever is true:" Culture talks about truth in a way that communicates that all truth is relative. As believers, we can be confident that not only is God's Word true, but our God Himself is Truth *(John 14:6)*. Meditate on and memorize Scripture. Think about who Jesus is and what He has done. Remember all the ways God has been faithful to you and to others in the past. Remind yourself how you've seen Him move in your life. Fill your mind with testimonies of others who know the Lord. Don't dwell on the lies, but be fascinated by His truth.

"whatever is honorable:" Sadly, it's much easier to find bad news than good news. From actual news channels to your social media feed, you'll likely come across more tragedy and anger than celebration and encouragement. There's no way to escape the brokenness of the world, but you can stop being surprised the world is broken. Jesus came, died and rose again so He can one day restore the world back to how it was before sin. Dwell on that instead of the world's brokenness.

"whatever is just:" Fellow high-justice friends, I feel you. It's hard to let go of things that are unfair. However, life being unfair is just another reality of living in a broken world. Plus, if we're being honest, dwelling on what is unfair often doesn't stop there. It's not a far leap to get to vengeance – which God says is His. For more encouragement for your heart on this, read Romans 12:17-21.

"whatever is pure:" The enemy has been spitting half-truths since the Garden of Eden. While half-truths may seem more innocent than blatant lies, they are every bit as dangerous. Half-truths are often culturally accepted because they sound good and appeal to our human logic and feelings. However, half-truths typically reduce a full truth about God and alter it enough to emphasize humanity over God, limiting both our worship and an accurate view of God. Be on guard against half-truths and diluted truth as much as you prepare yourself for the enemy's evil schemes.

"whatever is lovely:" You can be so consumed with worry that it limits your worship. You can become so aware of the brokenness of the world that you forget God created the world *(Genesis 1:1)* and God loves the world *(John 3:16)*. Take the time to watch the sun rise or set. If you love the ocean, allow yourself to be mesmerized by it. Hike a mountain and enjoy the view. Eat a good meal. Laugh with your friends. Use the gifts and abilities God has given you to serve others. Recognize that everything in your life – from the people in it to the breath in your lungs – is a gift from God. His goodness is matchless. Don't be so consumed by what's wrong that you can no longer see what is right.

"whatever is commendable:" There will always be something to criticize. But in the same way, there will always be something or someone you can encourage. Be wise in how you choose to use your time and use your words – including the ones you *think*, not just the ones you *say*. Think in a way that is congruent with encouragement, building others up and acknowledging what is good.

"whatever is excellent:" This is not grounds to ignore sin, but when you dwell on what is excellent, you are inclined to remember that through repentance and putting our faith in Jesus, we are restored to God through Christ's righteousness. Refusing to repent leads to shame, and repentance brings us back to where we started with God. Staying stuck in the shame cycle keeps you dwelling on yourself instead of dwelling on the Lord. Stay in awe of how Jesus saved you.

"whatever is praiseworthy:" Live a life of worship. Worship shouldn't be contained to a few songs on Sunday morning, but aim to live a life of praise. Everything you do can be done as worship. You can worship God through your work. You can worship God through moving your body in exercise. You can worship God through doing yet another load of laundry for your family. You can worship God through a date night with your spouse, cooking dinner for a family going through a hard time, or praying anytime the Holy Spirit prompts your heart. See God in everything, and recognize Him for everything.

Here's a quick chart to help you see both the positive and the negative in terms of evaluating what you think about:

SPIRAL UP (THINK ABOUT THESE THINGS)	SPIRAL DOWN (DO NOT THINK ABOUT)
what is true	what is false
what is honorable	what is corrupt
what is just	what is unfair
what is pure	what is diluted/contaminated
what is lovely	what is repulsive
what is commendable	what is wrong
what is excellent	what is shameful
what is praiseworthy	what is unworthy/common

4:9 *"Practice these things"* might be the three most encouraging words of this entire section. Thinking this way is not the normal cycle of the human brain. You may feel like you've allowed yourself to think about the wrong things for years *(maybe even decades!)* and you're unsure where to begin to change the direction of your spiral. Just like Paul says – put it into practice. Will you practice perfectly? No. But can you practice again after you mess up? Yes! Spiraling up takes practice, and most importantly, just as Paul comforts us in this verse, God's peace will be with you when you practice.

Paul gives four things to put into practice to help them change their thinking:

- *"learn:"* We live in a world that makes it possible to learn at the brush of our fingertips. Even when you don't mean to, a quick scroll of social media can cause you to "learn" many things. Evaluate what you're learning, how you're learning, and how that information affects you. As believers, the main growth we should be concerned with is becoming more like Christ. Is what you're learning making you more like Him?

CONVERSATIONAL COMMENTARY ON PHILIPPIANS

- *"receive:"* You can hear things without believing them. It's possible to hear a sermon or read a book like this one, even underlining as you go, without really receiving or believing what you're hearing/reading. What are you fully convinced is true – to the point of action, change and transformation?

- *"hear:"* Do the people you're listening to leave you more in awe of God or simply in awe of them? How many people are you listening to? You could actually be hearing all good content but end up paralyzed in action because there are simply too many voices in your life. Maybe you have good influences in your life, but you're also still listening to some voices that aren't so good for you either. Be careful what you hear. What we listen to has a greater effect than we often realize.

- *"see:"* Where are your eyes? Are you looking to Jesus and those He has put in your life who are walking with Him? Or are your eyes wandering – still curious about what the world has to offer you? In a similar way, are you being an example to the other believers in your life as we are called to do? (1 Timothy 4:12)

HOW TO SPIRAL UP
Learn *(What are you learning/studying?)*
Receive *(What do you really believe?)*
Hear *(Who/what are you listening to?)*
See *(Where are your eyes?)*

Philippians 4:1-9

QUESTIONS

Icebreaker: Think about the most joyful person you know. What makes them so joyful, and how do you feel when you're around them?

1. In Philippians 4:1, when Paul refers to the Philippians as his *"crown,"* he implies that he views their commitment to stand firm in the Lord as a crowning achievement – despite the fact that the church at Philippi didn't meet any of the measurements the world would deem as successful. What impact do you think it would have if every believer's greatest achievement involved the enduring faith of someone else? How do we change our definition of success to be more in line with what is modeled here?

2. Have you ever thought about how crazy it is to struggle with trusting God in your current circumstances while fully trusting Him for your eternity? Practically, what does it look like to allow your confidence in Christ and your hope in heaven to impact how you choose to live your faith today?

3. Read Philippians 4:2-3. How have you seen a disagreement between two people have a negative ripple effect on those around them? Considering what we know about these two women, why is it so important that they reconcile? What are some ways you've learned to lay down your opinion for the sake of the gospel? How do you think the world around us would be impacted if believers refused to divide over secondary and tertiary issues?

4. Do you think rejoicing is the reasonable response to what Jesus has done for us? In general, do you think that Christians are known for our joy? If you made no other changes to your life other than rejoicing in the Lord in everything, how would that affect your life and the lives of those around you? What do you think keeps us from living in the fullness of joy that's available to us in Jesus?

5. Read Philippians 4:6-7. Rejoicing in the Lord and turning our worries into prayers are two ways to reduce anxiety in our lives. If prayer brings the peace we long for, why do you think we expend so much energy searching for understanding instead of activating our faith? Practically, what steps can we take to put this truth into practice?

6. Read Philippians 4:8. Do you ever evaluate your thought life? Be honest with the group – what area(s) were you most challenged/ convicted about in terms of changing your thought life?

7. Which of the four things Paul encourages the Philippians to put into practice – *learn, receive, hear and see* – is the most difficult for you personally? Break into pairs and share how you need to be held accountable in this area and pray for each other.

Philippians 4:10-23

4:10 Just as Paul was grateful to God for the Philippians *(see commentary note on Philippians 1:3)*, Paul **"rejoices in the Lord"** that the Philippians were able to generously care for him. He is referring to the money Epaphroditus brought as a gift from the church at Philippi *(Philippians 2:25)*. Instead of highlighting Paul's gratitude for their gift, though, this verse indicates he was grateful they had an opportunity to be generous, since they *"were concerned for [him] but had no opportunity."* Generosity doesn't just bless the person on the receiving end; generosity blesses the giver. Your flesh will often view generosity as a sacrifice, but your soul is actually refreshed through generosity. When you have the opportunity to be generous, take it. Just as the Philippians were blessed, you will be also. *[See Proverbs 11:24-25, Luke 6:38 and 2 Corinthians 9:6-8 for more reminders of what Scripture says about generosity.]*

4:11 Depending on the translation you're reading from, it will either indicate Paul was not speaking from being **"in need"** or speaking **"from want."** In the western world, we distinguish between needs and wants, whereas to the Philippians, needs and wants were one in the same. Because of the way wide-spread affluence has affected us, **"from want"** is probably a more accurate translation for us to understand today what Paul was communicating then. If we do not learn to be content, we will think, speak and act out of discontentment – aka *from want.* That's why three of the most encouraging words from this verse should be that phrase *"I have learned."* Discontentment is natural; *contentment* is something we must learn. Paul's current circumstance is proof these words are true. He is encouraging the church at Philippi *(and all of us thousands of years later!)* from behind bars. Prison, though it was not an ideal circumstance, did not steal from Paul's joy in Jesus or zeal for the gospel mission.

Because discontentment is natural, you may not even notice the warning signs that you are discontent. You may need to learn to be content if you struggle with a combination of the warning signs below:

WARNING SIGNS OF DISCONTENTMENT

EXTREME EXHAUSTION:	WILLINGNESS TO COMPROMISE YOUR CHARACTER/WITNESS:
• When you want more, you end up working all the time and trying to do too much. • *Proverbs 23:4*	• When the "ends justify the means" for the potential to gain more, it can become easier + easier to rationalize corrupt behavior. • *Proverbs 15:27*
INTENSE WORRY/ANXIETY:	**HAMSTER WHEEL OF SATISFACTION:**
• The more you have, the more you will have to worry about. *(How will I invest, maintain, care for, save, pay taxes, fix when broken, protect against being stolen, etc.)* • *Ecclesiastes 5:11-12 (Current studies prove Solomon's observation in these verses: The greater the income, the greater the insomnia.)*	• Believing more of something will satisfy you, getting it yet not being satisfied, then switching your striving to more of something else to satisfy you over and over again... • *Ecclesiastes refers to this as "chasing the wind" in nearly every chapter. For a deep dive on this book that really helps understand the power of the gospel in the midst of a broken world, see Conversational Commentary on Ecclesiastes: Wisdom to Live for Heaven while on Earth.*
HIGH STRESS (MIND + BODY):	
• Hard work + poor sleep has a cost – emotionally *or physically. We're humans with limits, and stress will inevitably catch up with you. My friend, Donna Gibbs, always reminds me that the body keeps score.* • *Proverbs 14:30*	

After the commentary, prior to the group discussion questions, you'll find a guided reflection + prayer time to dig deep into learning to be content. Before you go any further in this study, I'd encourage you to flip to page 84 now to complete that exercise. Feel free to keep your takeaways between you and the Lord, but if you desire extra accountability and encouragement, you will have an opportunity to share your reflection with your group.

4:12   Spoiler alert: the *"secret"* Paul refers to here is Jesus. He does not speak hypothetically either. Paul had experienced seasons of great wealth, prosperity and success in his life. He also experienced hunger and what the NASB translation refers to as *"suffering need"* (such as his current circumstance in prison) where he was at the mercy of the generosity of others to cover his basic needs like food and clothing. Whether he had much or hardly anything at all, Paul realized that the only way he would actually be content is if he continued to look to Jesus for security and significance. This is a similar sentiment that David shared when he wrote, **"Because your steadfast love is better than life, my lips will praise You"** (Psalm 63:3). Are you in a season of serious struggle and suffering? Cling to Jesus. He is all you need. Are you in a season of abundance and victory? Your response should be the same as it is in suffering. Jesus is all you need. Cling to Jesus, not the abundance. Cling to Jesus, not the need. No matter what your circumstance is, Christ is sufficient to be your contentment. Otherwise, you'll head right for the hamster wheel of satisfaction. Examine the radical difference between these two statements:

The Secret of Learning to Be Content:

- **World's Way:** focus on what you don't have that you want to get and can't keep

- **Christ's Way:** focus on what you need that you have and cannot lose *(Jesus)*

Jesus is your significance. Jesus is your security. Going anywhere else for your foundational needs is idolatry.

4:13   This is a verse that is frequently shared out of context. It's a powerful verse, and it's absolutely one to memorize and meditate on... but it's not about your ability or what you are able to accomplish. This verse continues the conversation about contentment in Christ. Often, when this verse is shared in isolation, it's used in the context that refers to some form of impressive accomplishment, whether that's scoring a touchdown at the big game or winning the highest award. But it's really important that we remember that *"all things"* is exactly what it says – *all. things.* BIG THINGS, small things, hard things, easy things, things I desire to do, things I *don't* desire to do, known things, unknown things, scary things, exciting things, sacrificial things... **All things** are possible when Jesus is our power Source. Through the strength of Christ, you can remain steadfast in faith with full joy – whether you win or lose, on the mountain top or deepest valley, both in exceeding abundance or suffering need. When you are full of Christ – the only thing that you truly need – you won't want for anything else. Jesus, in His rightful place in your life, as the One who is unchanging and eternal, will outweigh every other earthly desire that is ever-changing and temporary.

Our flesh tends to do everything we can independently and only come to God at the end of our ability. However, that mindset is drastically short-sighted. Even life's simple things are possible because of God's goodness and grace. Let's do a quick exercise: Take a few deep breaths. Pretty simple, right? After all, you breathe 24/7, mostly subconsciously. But in reality, God is the Source for those few simple breaths you just took. God knit together your lungs when He knit every part of you in your mother's womb *(Psalm 139:13)*. He put breath in your lungs *(Genesis 2:7)*. When He did those things, He thought of everything, like making it possible for you to keep breathing when you sleep or simply stop thinking about it. You don't merely need God for the hard, the broken and the impossible. You need Him just as much in the easy, the simple, and the everyday. When you find yourself praising Him less for the simple things He does in and through you *(or maybe not even thinking of Him at all)*, it's as if you're taking the credit for something you simply didn't do.

Remember how Paul used the language of *"practice these things"* in Philippians 4:9? The practice continues here. Practice drifting toward gratitude instead of discontentment. When you find yourself drifting to speak out of want, enjoy what you have through gratitude instead. In the moments when the only thing you have to enjoy is Jesus, dwell on your confidence that God sent Him to save you and that His work on the cross counts as your righteousness. When you do that, *"only having Jesus"* will never feel like less. It will feel like everything – because it is.

4:14   Although Paul fully relies on Christ, he is grateful for the way the Philippians have cared for him during his time of need. In his letter to the church at Galatia, Paul reminds them of the importance of *"bearing one another's burdens to fulfill the law of Christ"* (Galatians 6:2). Part of loving one another is to *"share in afflictions with one another"* as the church at Philippi did for Paul. However, the reality that God is all we need does not give us simultaneous permission to live independently from one another, assuming God's provision would not include using us to minister to one another.

The way God has called us to live calls us to:

- outdo one another in showing honor *(Romans 12:10)*
- to serve one another *(1 Peter 2:10)*
- to encourage one another and build each other up *(1 Thessalonians 5:11)*
- to meet one another's needs *(Romans 12:13)* – just to name a few.

What are some ways that you can share in others' afflictions in your life right now? Pray for God to reveal those things and obey where He leads you.

4:15-16   To put a more concrete timeline to the words Paul uses here, this indicates that from Acts 16 on, the Philippians were the only ones to financially support Paul's missionary journeys. Even when Paul was in Thessolonica, which Biblical scholars say could have been as short as three weeks or as long as three months, the Philippians sent him multiple gifts to support the short-term gospel work he was doing there. Between all the churches

Paul started, it's hard to imagine the Philippians being the only church willing to financially contribute toward him being able to do what he had done for them somewhere else. Yet, it's consistent with human behavior you've likely encountered on your own and stories shared in Scripture. For example, consider the ten lepers Jesus healed in Luke 17:11-19. Ten lepers were healed, and yet, only one turned back to praise God and thank Jesus for His healing. Who really missed out here? Not Jesus – He didn't need their thanks, but in not coming back, the other nine neglected the opportunity to praise God and grow their faith. God promises to supply all of our needs. *(Paul will share that truth when we get to 4:19!)* He will always provide for His work to be done, but you and I can miss out on the opportunity to be a part of it and fail to experience the blessing of a growing faith and relationship with Him. Giving financially is a necessary and beautiful way to participate in the work of the ministry being done around you.

4:17   Paul is not after their gift. He is after the spiritual fruit that he knows will be made possible by their generosity. Paul acknowledges that their provision for him paved the way for people to accept the gospel, for new churches to be planted, and for young churches to continue to receive care and discipleship from Paul. By saying that the *"fruit increases to your credit,"* Paul reminds them that though they may not be present for all of the work he is doing, they are responsible for the gospel wins he's seeing. Consequently, they will one day be rewarded by God for how they contributed to Paul's ministry. Three important applications for us:

- Desire spiritual fruit above gifts.
- Expand your gospel influence by contributing financially when you are able, even if you cannot give of your time or be there to see the fruit reaped.
- In Kingdom work, you don't give something to get something. God will reward you. Comparing the two, you do not want to settle for an earthly reward.

4:18   These words have lost some of their rich meaning in our culture today, which is why it's important to read Scripture in a way that remembers what the words would have meant to the culture when Paul was writing. Phrases like *"fragrant offering"* and *"acceptable and pleasing sacrifice to God"* point back to the Old Testament practices of making sacrifices before God. There were many rules that regulated these sacrifices, but no matter how wealthy or how poor you were, what was customary for you to sacrifice before God was just that – a sacrifice. Traditional Old Testament sacrifices weren't based on what was comfortable for your budget but what demonstrated to God that you were serious about your repentance for your sin. While Jesus was the full payment for sin that satisfied, giving to God's work can align your heart posture in a similar way that sacrifices did in the Old Testament. If we do not give in a way that is sacrificial and puts God at the center, we will default to giving *(or not giving!)* in a way that is selfish and puts ourselves at the center.

4:19-20: After an extensive conversation on giving, Paul reminds us of the reason why we can give sacrificially to others: While you take care of others, God takes care of you. Again, it is important to distinguish the use of the word *"needs"* here. Paul's not about sharing a "you-scratch-God's-back-and-He'll-scratch-yours" theology. But in sending Jesus to die for our sins in our place as the perfect sacrifice, to defeat death, so He can one day return for the saints, God has already delivered on this promise. Loop back to Philippians 4:11-13. Jesus is all we need to the glory of God the Father. And please don't miss that last, powerful word: Amen. Most believers say *"Amen"* only at the conclusion of a prayer – *"Amen"* actually means *"truly"* or *"so be it."* Every time you say *"Amen,"* it is a declaration of your faith in what God has already done and will do.

Say this out loud: "God will supply all my needs through Jesus to His glory forever. So be it!"

Let that be your attitude in giving and generosity.

4:21-22 It's easy to check out early when you're reading Paul's letters. What could possibly be missed as he says goodbye? Well, as far as these two verses go, a lot could be missed! Paul refers to every saint – all of those who make up the church at Philippi and all of the believers who are with Paul. But Paul does make one specific distinction – the saints who are of Caesar's household greet the Philippians. Without going into all the details, Paul's words let us know that even in prison under Caesar's guard, the gospel is going forward among the very people who are holding him captive! *(If that doesn't make you jump up and down, at least figuratively, check your pulse!)* No matter how dire or impossible your circumstances seem, there is no place where the gospel cannot move. God's mission is that powerful! Stay steadfast. Stay joyful. He is always working, and through Jesus, God invites each one of us to be part of His work in the world!

4:23   Grace is the driving force of every word Paul has written and every application to follow – then and now. You cannot muster up His grace on your own. It flows from Jesus, and His wells never run dry. When you feel like your grace tank is empty – *and listen, I've said it before too, and even though it always gets a giggle* – you're really only exposing the truth that you're running on your own supply of grace instead of relying on His. Letting His grace **"be with your spirit"** is Paul's way of reminding the Philippians *(and us!)* to let God's grace be the deepest part of who you are and aim to be. Aim for grace, and you'll always land on Jesus.

LEARNING TO BE CONTENT

GUIDED REFLECTION
+ PRAYER JOURNAL

Contentment. It's a word we are familiar with, but a feeling that is all too easy to come and go. In Philippians 4:11, Paul writes words that bring me so much comfort: *"I am not saying this because I am in need, for **I have learned to be content** whatever the circumstances."* Paul *learned* to be content. Contentment is not natural; it is learned.

If you look for contentment in your circumstances or what the world has to offer, you will constantly encounter reminders of what you *don't* have – which explains why contentment is something that's hard to keep, even if you can get it for a little while. In the following pages, I'm praying you'll have the courage to write down what is distracting you from learning contentment and focus on Whose you are and everything He has graciously given you.

Lord, help us to learn to be content. We trust You.

In Him,
Michelle

DISCONTENTMENT BRAIN DUMP

In case you've never done one before, brain dumps are really simple. Don't overthink it. As quickly and as unfiltered as you can, simply write down all the things that you think of that can cause you to battle discontentment. *(Reminder: this exercise will only be as helpful as you are honest!)*

SURRENDER

When I did the exercise above, I couldn't believe some of the things I wrote down. Some were really serious. Others were embarrassing to admit. As it always goes with a brain dump, I was all over the map – you probably were too. But after examining my list, I realized that everything I had written down fit into just two categories: something I must give to God *(ex - a loved one with an illness)* or a lie that isn't from Him *(ex - feeling unqualified for what He's called me to do)*.

Go ahead and try it with your list below:

GIVE TO GOD	LIES

RENEW YOUR MIND

It's time to replace the lies you identified with truth. For the lies that can really cripple you, I recommend looking up Scripture you can read and re-read. But at the very least, write down what you know is true instead of the lie.

LIE	TRUTH

PRAYER

Use this space how it will be most helpful for you. If you want to rewrite the things you need to give to God and the truths you need to renew your mind with as prayer prompts, and spend some time in prayer, do that. Or if you process better on paper, you can write down your prayer to the Lord.

_____

_____

_____

LEARN TO BE CONTENT

Read these verses aloud. Really think about what they mean. Underline/circle words that stand out to you. You can use the following blank pages to write down what the Lord shows you as you learn to be content. (This is certainly not an exhaustive list – but a great start!)

"I know what it is to be in need, and I know what it is to have plenty. I have learned the secret of being content in any and every situation, whether well fed or hungry, whether living in plenty or in want. I can do all this through Him who gives me strength." - Philippians 4:11-13

"It is the Lord who goes before you. He will be with you; he will not leave you or forsake you. Do not fear or be dismayed." - Deuteronomy 31:8

"My mouth will tell of your righteous acts, of your deeds of salvation all the day, for their number is past my knowledge. With the mighty deeds of the Lord God I will come; I will remind them of Your righteousness, Yours alone." - Psalm 71:15-16

"For the love of money is a root of all kinds of evil. Some people, eager for money, have wandered from the faith and pierced themselves with many griefs. But you, man of God, flee from all this, and pursue righteousness, godliness, faith, love, endurance and gentleness." - 1 Timothy 6:10-11

"I have been crucified with Christ; and it is no longer I who live, but Christ lives in me; and the life which I now live in the flesh I live by faith in the Son of God, who loved me and gave Himself up for me." - Galatians 2:20

"That is why, for Christ's sake, I delight in weaknesses, in insults, in hardships, in persecutions, in difficulties. For when I am weak, then I am strong." - 2 Corinthians 12:10

"For our sake He made Him to be sin who knew no sin, so that in Him we might become the righteousness of God." - 2 Corinthians 5:21

"But godliness with contentment is great gain. For we brought nothing into the world, and we can take nothing out of it." - 1 Timothy 6:6-7

"The Lord is not slow to fulfill his promise as some count slowness, but is patient toward you, not wishing that any should perish, but that all should reach repentance." - 2 Peter 3:9

"Keep your lives free from the love of money and be content with what you have, because God has said, 'Never will I leave you; never will I forsake you.'" - Hebrews 13:5

A PRAYER WHEN I
BATTLE DISCONTENTMENT

Lord, I need You.
Guide my eyes to see Your goodness.
Guard my mind to remember Your grace.
Fill my ears with Your truth,
And help my mouth overflow with Your praise.
Firmly fixed on Jesus,
Keep me in step with Your Spirit.

Father, Your presence alone comforts me.
But I confess that I still fight my flesh's desire for lesser things.
I know they are empty pursuits,
That they will never satisfy.
But in my weakness,
I get curious.
I get distracted.
I get discontent.
Forgive me.

Thank You for protecting me,
For loving me so fiercely,
For always providing me a way out
When I am tempted to want what You haven't given me.
God, I desire for You to be my only desire.
Help me to make You my one desire.

Keep me in awe of what You've done,
Instead of dwelling on what I haven't done.
Remind me of all I have in You,
Instead of being reminded of what I don't have.
Show me who You are over and over again,
So I will stop being consumed with myself.

Teach me to be content.
I trust You to teach me.
Make me more like Jesus.
I love You.
Amen.

Philippians 4:10-23

QUESTIONS

_____

Icebreaker: What do you think most people in today's culture believe would bring them contentment?

1. Verse 10 provides us with the reminder that generosity is not just a blessing for the one who receives but for the one who gives. Our flesh sees generosity as a sacrifice, but the soul knows generosity as a blessing. Have different group members volunteer to read the passages below, then discuss what each verse reminds us about generosity from God's perspective. What do you miss out on when you have an opportunity to be generous and you do not take it?

    - _Proverbs 11:24-25_

    - _Luke 6:3_

    - _2 Corinthians 9:6-8_

2. Read Philippians 4:11. How does Paul's perspective that contentment is learned both encourage you and challenge you? Review the chart about the warning signs of discontentment, then have each group member share which warning sign hit them hardest personally. [If your group is willing to share takeaways from their guided reflection and prayer time on discontentment, you can also take time to discuss here.]

3. The commentary note on Philippians 4:12 challenges you to examine the radical difference between the secret of learning to be content the world's way _(focusing on what you don't have that you want to get and can't keep)_ vs. Christ's way _(focusing on what you need that you have and cannot lose – Jesus)._ Discuss the difference practically between what it looks like to pursue Christ's way of contentment instead of the world's way.

4. Read Philippians 4:11-13 together. Philippians 4:13 is about so much more than our ability or achievements, but shows that when our contentment is wrapped up in Christ, we live in such a way that acknowledges Him as our Source of power and strength for all things. A reflective question to discover what you rely on as your life's perspective, priority and power source is your answer to the two questions below. Take some time to think about them as a group. If your answer to both questions is not Christ, you are relying on an inferior power source. Take a moment to confess to God and one another the inferior power sources you can be drawn to in place of Jesus.

    • What are you drawn to when you feel empty inside?

    • What are you drawn to when you are fully satisfied?

5. Philippians 4:4-18 highlight some powerful truths about generosity. Using the principles highlighted in the passage and commentary, discuss these questions:

    • Based on what you learned in these verses, is generosity an act of worship? How?

    • How does your generosity affect your relationship with God? With others?

    • What are some challenges we may face in being generous, and how can we overcome them?

    • If an act of giving is not sacrificial, is it generosity? Why or why not?

    • Who all gets blessed by one act of generosity?

6. Read Philippians 4:11-13 and 4:19-20 aloud as one continuous thought. Have the person reading replace *"Amen"* with *"so be it!"* as they read. How should it impact your contentment and generosity – and your faith in general – to remember how God has already delivered on His promise through Jesus? What are practical ways we can remind ourselves and others of this truth both in word and action?

7. Because God's grace was the deepest part of who Paul aimed to be, God was able to use his imprisonment to win some of Caesar's household to believe in the gospel. The commentary note on Philippians 4:23 put it this way: "Grace is the driving force of every word Paul has written and every application to follow – then and now. You cannot muster His grace up on your own. It flows from Jesus, and His wells never run dry. When you feel like your grace tank is empty – *and listen, I've said it before too, and even though it always gets a giggle* – you're really only exposing the truth that you're running on your own supply of grace instead of relying on His." Are you running on His supply of grace in your spirit or trying to muster it up on your own? Based on everything you've learned in studying Philippians, what are some practical ways you can let His grace be with your spirit in every circumstance moving forward?

Recommended Books & Resources

FOR DEEPER STUDY

Strong's Exhaustive Concordance of the Bible
Strong, James. *The New Strong's Exhaustive Concordance of the Bible : With Main Concordance, Appendix to the Main Concordance, Hebrew and Aramaic Dictionary of the Old Testament, Greek Dictionary of the New Testament.* Nashville Tenn., T. Nelson, 1997.

The Expositor's Bible Commentary Ephesians, Philippians, Colossians, Philemon
Longman, Tremper, et al. *The Expositor's Bible Commentary: Ephesians-Philemon.* Zondervan, 2006.

Christ-Centered Exposition Series
Merida, Tony. *Christ-Centered Exposition: Exalting Jesus in Ecclesiastes.* Nashville, TN, Holman Reference, 2016.

The ESV Study Bible
Crossway Bibles. *ESV : Study Bible : English Standard Version.* Wheaton, Ill., Crossway Bibles, 2016.

Systematic Theology by Wayne Grudem
Grudem, Wayne A. *Systematic Theology.* Grand Rapids, Mich., Zondervan, 1994.

The Visual Word by Patrick Schreiner
Schreiner, Patrick, and Anthony M Benedetto. The *Visual Word : Illustrated Outlines of the New Testament Books.* Chicago, Moody Publishers, 2021.

ESV Story of Redemption Bible
Not Available. *HOLY BIBLE: English Standard Version, Story of Redemption Bible.* Crossway, 2018.

Pocket Dictionary of Theological Terms (Grenz, Guretzki + Nordling)
Grenz, Stanley J, et al. *Pocket Dictionary of Theological Terms.* Downers Grove, Ill., Intervarsity Press, 1999.

Dictionary of Paul and His Letters

Hawthorne, Gerald F., et al. *Dictionary of Paul and His Letters a Compendium of Contemporary Biblical Scholarship.* InterVarsity Press, 2015.

Be Joyful: Even When Things Go Wrong, You Can Have Joy

Wiersbe, Warren W. *Be Joyful: Even When Things Go Wrong, You Can Have Joy.* David C. Cook, 2008.

To Live Is Christ to Die Is Gain

Chandler, Matt. *To Live Is Christ to Die Is Gain.* David C Cook Publishing Company, 2014.

Bible Project: Philippians

BibleProject. *"Book of Philippians: Guide with Key Information and Resources."* BibleProject, 13 Sept. 2023, bibleproject.com/guides/book-of-philippians/.

SWHW

SHE WORKS HIS WAY

She Works His Way is dedicated to building
a gospel-centered discipleship community to resource,
equip and encourage women to do their God-given work
for the glory of God and the benefit of His church.

SHEWORKSHISWAY.COM

f /sheworkshisway   @sheworkshisway

Listen on Spotify   Listen on Apple Podcasts

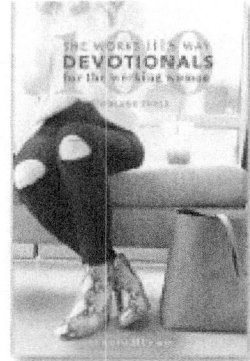

SHEWORKSHISWAY.COM/SHOP

Printed in Great Britain
by Amazon

38999011R00059